YOU CAN DO THIS!

HOW TO SUCCEED
IN SALES
AND IN LIFE

BY
ADRIAN N.
HAVELOCK

RSPE
GROUP

For the people who inspired me
the most my whole life in pursuing my goals.
I dedicate this book to my parents
Mr and Mrs Clifton and Joyce Havelock.

REVIEWS

YOU CAN DO THIS!

Everyone needs encouragement. *Everyone*. Even the greatest and most courageous people we see are still emotionally needy in some ways at some times. As are you and I. It is in those moments that we thirst for and seek approval or encouragement. The problem is that most people don't know how to provide it. They say things like, "Oh, I'm sure it will work out OK." or "Just stay positive." Or "It will be fine." That's not encouragement. That's reassurance. It's no more than saying, "Yes, this is the correct path."

Those statements don't achieve what encouragement should achieve: an **increase in courage**. In other words, to "en-courage" means to stimulate more courage in the person. For that to be achieved much more than reassurance is necessary. For example, you may say, "I've seen you do things like this before. You are strong enough and smart enough to figure this out. "You Can Do This!": now that is encouraging!

Adrian N. Havelock has done all of us a good service by writing this book. He has told his own story, boldly, frankly and openly. Plus, he has assembled the proven wisdom that is practiced by all high achievers. This book is a simple, enjoyable journey through the thinking and the actions that we all must follow in order to become successful.

I encourage you to follow his guidance and let yourself flow through the exercises and skills in this book. You will be better, stronger, faster and much more confident once you do this. Believe me, I've worked with hundreds of thousands of people around the world and I know this works. The system works, the skills matter, the steps are laid out clearly and you can do this!

In the Spirit of Growth,
Jim Cathcart, CSP, CPAE

Jim Cathcart is a Hall of Fame Professional Speaker and author of 18 books, including *Relationship Selling* and *The Self-Motivation Handbook*. Cathcart is also the founder of Cathcart.com.

ACKNOWLEDGEMENTS

I would like to take this opportunity to recognise a few people who have significantly contributed to this book. They have all encouraged me, given me words of encouragement and advice. They have checked in with me when I slacked off and they have given me motivation when I hit a milestone. I have a lot of support from many other people, but I am unable to list all of them here as it would be too much to keep track of. Since you are reading this, I encourage you to let the world know.

I want to say a special thank you to:

- Tony J. Selimi, best-selling author of *#Loneliness and A Path to Wisdom* and mentor to world famous executives.
- Andy Harrington, *Sunday Times* best-selling author of *Passion into Profit* and world's number one public speaking expert.

- Jim Cathcart, best-selling author of 18 books including *The Acorn Principle* and *Relationship Selling* and inductee into the Sales and Marketing hall of fame 2012.
- Romeo Effs, author *of Enthusiasm Unchained and Serial Entrepreneur.*
- Robert Rolih, Amazon best-selling author of *The Million Dollar Decision* and mentor on *What the Financial Industry Doesn't Want You to Know.*
- Nienke Van Bezooijen, author of *The Speaker Success Solution* and owner at Presentation Master.
- Clint Arjoon, entrepreneur and owner of Trinidad Blocks Company Limited.
- Nigel R. Khan, entrepreneur and owner of the Nigel R. Khan Booksellers chain of stores.

Additional thank you to:

- Jaishree Misir, my wife for her support in my entrepreneurial journey from the very start.
- The late and great John Von Achen for his support and advice when I began planning how to write my book.

- The late and great Angelo Bissessarsingh, an honoured and well-loved historian and researcher.

List of inspirational people who inspire me to achieve great things in this world and don't even know that they do it:

- Anthony Robbins
- Darren Hardy
- Les Brown
- Robin Sharma
- Oprah Winfrey
- Richard Branson
- Dalai Lama
- Mark Gungor
- Nick Vujicic
- The late and great Jim Rohn

List of business colleagues and groups who inspired and encouraged me during my journey:

- Richard Lewis
- David Lewis
- Fareez Taariq Mohammed

- Wesley Hadeed
- Christiansen Ian Smith
- The Cash Flow Club of Trinidad and Tobago and its members
- The Rotary Clubs in Trinidad and Tobago and its members in the various clubs
- Judy Alcantara and 'Fit For Life'
- Anthony A. Chadee

All my family, friends and people I've worked with and trained who are too many to list but know who they are. Your words of encouragement inspired me to keep pushing.

Thank you. Thank you. Thank you!

CONTENTS

PREFACE

At the age of 19, I started my first real job as a salesman at Bavarian Motors Limited, the local BMW franchaise in Trinidad and Tobago. Perhaps the directors saw something in me when they decided to give me a shot at the job. This is where my passion for sales began.

Within two years I was in the top three in sales in the country for the BMW brand. Ever since, I have used techniques that I've learnt from others as well as through many types of training on how to interact with customers. Most importantly, I gained significant experience and developed my own techniques which I found very effective in harnessing my business skills.

In my book, you will learn these same techniques in order to grow your own business whether you're a sales person or small business owner. My techniques are more in alignment with finding new businesses or people in organisations to work with rather than performing marketing functions by rote. However, the communication techniques that are included in this book give you the information needed to be more effective in selling to new customers.

Although this book is about succeeding in sales and in life, I must say some of the techniques you will come across, perhaps you've known them already or perhaps it may be new to you. In any type of sales training or sales book, there will be similar techniques and experiences shared. I do hope my experiences, as well as those of others that are included in the book, will be of significant value to you.

Sincerely,

Adrian N. Havelock

CHAPTER 1

THE SUCCESS MINDSET

"Today, you have the opportunity to transcend from a disempowered mind-set of existence, to an empowered reality of purpose-driven living. Today is a new day that has been handed to you for shaping. You have the tools, now get out there and create a masterpiece."

~Steve Maraboli

Clint is a family friend of mine. At the age of 11 he said to himself that he didn't want to have a boss. Here is a short story told by him, someone I know personally, who lives in a developing country. What I mean by 'developing country' is a country or nation seeking to become more advanced economically, technologically and socially. There is, however, no universal, agreed-upon criterion for what makes a country developing versus developed. Although, GDP per capita is an example of a reference point that is used. Basically, developing countries are those that are growing.

The island of Trinidad and Tobago in the Caribbean is the economic hub and business centre of the Caribbean. Rich in oil and natural gas, it also has a large manufacturing sector and in 2011, the Organisation for Economic Co-operation and Development (OECD) removed Trinidad and Tobago from its list of Developing Countries.

When Clint was a young boy, he first learned to make a profit purchasing bicycle handle flyers and cheese cloth at the local market whenever his parents would go, and return to the village to resell them. This was his first hand at business. He got them for 0.99 cents and sold them for $3.00. At that time there weren't many cars around and he was lucky enough to have access to one to be able to make those trips. Clint and I sat down one Monday evening and he shared a story about his life that I believe is one of the most interesting uses of human interaction, communication techniques, and most importantly, persistence. Clint created his life around the things he wanted to achieve. That is, success!

Here's the story as told by him:

"Growing up, my eldest brother used to do woodworking (carpentry). I observed what my brother used to do with the wood, it's where I learnt to make coffee tables and trollies and I would sell them. By the age of 14, I started planting vegetables so that I could sell them in the market. By 16, I finished high school and decided I wanted to buy my first car within one year. I had my eyes set on a Mazda 626 Coupe. Unfortunately, although pushing as hard as possible, I was unable to achieve that. It did not deter me though, in fact, it fuelled my passion towards obtaining other things. Because I came really close to making it happen!

In 1985, I started working in the oilfields helping my dad as a runner boy, because I knew to myself that I wanted to work and build a family business. I thought that by doing this I would be gaining experience in as many fields as possible. By 1989 I was able to save enough money to buy my first used car, and from there, I started a rental company that became very successful! This led me to own six cars by the end of that same year! That was one of the most successful times I experienced back then. For three years I managed that company until I decided to shut it down, because I needed a change and, it was also a time when the country was beginning to face a recession.

After a brief and unsuccessful attempt to migrate to New York and realising how lonely life would be, I returned to Trinidad to work in the oilfields where I managed the operations of a company in that industry for five years. While there, I began purchasing chemicals for farmers because I observed that all the farmers in the village had to travel long distances to purchase their agro supplies. As the business started to quickly grow, I was able to sell not just chemicals, but everything related to agro supplies. I then opened an agro shop in 1992. This was one of my largest business decisions at the time as I then ended up having two locations! At the second location located in a nearby village called Dow Village, South Oropouche, I used to sit everyday admiring an abandoned property on a corner lot nearby. In fact, it was a really nice spot. I visualised myself working there, having ownership of it, and thought about that every day because it was always right in front of me. I saw possibilities. I saw so many things I could do. It kept 'calling my name'. But I did not have the money to purchase it. I only had enough to run the small business."

I digress from Clint's story at this time since I want you to get into his mind, and try to see what he sees, and how he sees it. More so, why he is seeing these things in that way? If you didn't realise it yet, Clint basically overlooked obstacles and only focused on opportunities. He has a wealth of experience in many different ventures, and up to this day, especially looking at the ones that did not work out, he never saw any of them as failures. But why? Let's continue:

> *"One day, I decided that I wanted to go to a car drag racing event. Whilst there, I was standing under some tents as a spectator and realised how quickly the tents were dismantled whenever the teams were packing up. The thought occurred to me, "This looks like I can make some money with this." Without hesitation, I decided I was going to explore such a business idea. By the Friday of the same week, I had owned a 10x10 tent to learn more about it, and see what it was like. Early in 1996, I thought about a company name for this new business that would have been <u>powerful</u>, and registered the company "Trinidad Tent Rentals Ltd". I registered the company and I didn't even have any stock as yet!*

> *Over the following six months, I was persistent in meeting with all the banks in Trinidad to obtain a loan. I'm sure you know where this is going when I tell you that, not one of them granted me a loan. Through months of sheer determination to access a loan, I returned to Republic Bank where one loan officer gave me the opportunity. I only got this because I also had a start-off figure of $5,000.00 and a security from a small business development company as a guarantor. In total, I secured a loan for the amount of $80,000.00.*

What I did next was pretty profound because I purchased all the tent tops from the United States and manufactured the entire framework for myself at home. On the 1ˢᵗ August of 1996, I actually had my first customer, who rented it for a charity event in the village. My contribution to the event was a significantly reduced price.

Adrian, to this day, I believe that starting off this business working with a charity was a major stepping stone in life! At the end of 1997 I was able to purchase the property that was located at the Agro Shop's second location. Goal achieved!"

Today, Clint is the number one supplier in the country for portable washrooms for construction, has a block factory and many real estate properties working for him.

He is a director in the Rotary Club, along with myself and has been serving others for the past 15 years.

Now look at his thought process, look at the way in which he thinks, the belief he had in himself and what he achieved. Look at how he overcame obstacles that were in his way, environmental factors, people, institutions.

It's no longer the question of "how did he do it?" but "why don't we work like that in achieving our goals?" Too many times we see what can go wrong and let that stop us. Too many times we try once or twice and fail, and let that stop us. Too many times we are not inspired enough to push through countless failures to achieve what we want in life!

"Excellence is not a skill, it's an attitude"

~Ralph Marston

Although this book is about the effective communication techniques used in the sales process, we first need to understand the mind-set of successful people. In fact, I'd like to say, 'the super-successful people'. We need to get into the mind-set, understand how they think, why they think this way and what motivates them to be a success. In order to be successful at anything, especially when it comes to obtaining new business, we need to do just as successful people do. It's not about copying what they do, anyone can copy and put on a disguise. Really understanding how it works is what will help us to become even better persons than we presently are right now.

In this chapter, you will realise that I am focusing on you. You won't be reading content about sales, communication or any types of strategies. I want you to focus on where *you* are now and look at yourself in the next year, five years or even 10 years from now. Who is the person you want to become? I advise that you participate in the following paragraphs you'll be reading and to take special note of the exercises I have for you. By the end of this chapter, you will have the mind-set of someone ready to take on any challenge that comes your way. Write in this book. Underline or highlight anything that jumps out at you. Photocopy a page and keep it on you at all times or snap it and save it to your mobile device. This is your guide, your new business bible.

Please note, that in this chapter, the content is interactive and in a way, has a real-time flow and feel.

THE PEAK PERFORMER

As human beings, I believe that we group people into two areas. The 1% successful, and the 99% average human being. The reason I am giving you two groups is the way in which I want to emphasise a difference. I am not here to discriminate nor look down on anyone. We are all human, we are all loving creatures and we live interdependent of one another. I just want to show a difference with the successful people and the rest of us. Just to reassure you, remember, you are an amazing person. You are you, and no one can take away your qualities, your skills and your abilities. I believe in you!

Let's shift focus onto what I really want to talk about, and that's the top 1% successful people. The Bill Gates', the Bransons', the Tony Robbins' and Elon Musks' of the world. No, I am not going to talk about their wealth, health, success, or who they know. I am going to focus on their minds. I want to show you what I have learnt from observing all of these people. I want to let you see what I see, and learn what I do when I interact with them, work with them and hang out with them.

Now, if you think I am going to talk about being positive and think that, *this book is not going to be interesting!* You've read all of those things already; but my perspective is different. It's going to be more strategy rather than me just telling you that positive thinking works. Strategy is the key to understanding not only how to be positive, but also how to be happy, enjoy your life and what you do. I agree that a positive mind set is tantamount to a successful life. It goes hand-in-hand with hard work.

Chris Gardner, the author of *The Pursuit of Happyness* once said, "Whatever you do, don't do it for the income, do it for the outcome". Read that line again (I recommend the book by the way).

Successful people do it for themselves. They do whatever they do because it gives them inner peace and a good feeling inside. Based on our present circumstances, and what we presently do, let's ask the question, "does it make me feel good inside?" If not, decide what you want to do and pursue it. You can and you will find a way to monetise it if you take the necessary action steps.

> "Excellence is the gradual result of
> always striving to do better"
> **~Pat Riley**

We need a strategy for pursuing what makes us feel good. Having that dream job, running that company, increasing your sales significantly, or even getting that special someone. The strategies in this book will help you in any of those areas.

We need to understand that in anything we do, because we are human beings, we are interdependent on one another. There is no one successful person who didn't have the help or influence of others. I mean that! How would they make money if there was no one to pay? Have you ever seen a rich hermit? In discussing a **peak performer**, we first need to understand what I mean by those two words.

The **peak performer** is the type of person who considers themselves an expert. I should ask you, think about this, are you an expert at something? It does not have to be work related. Are you really good at cooking, painting, driving or anything else?

Think about what you're good at for a moment. Great! Now don't you feel good about yourself?

A **peak performer** is someone who thinks above 'just success', by demanding more of themselves. They demand more from themselves because of the way in which they identify themselves. They identify themselves as someone who is passionately connected to something that drives them to succeed. This is why they are always inspired to do more, achieve more and serve more.

I want you to spend the next five minutes making a list in the workbook spaces provided. Make as many notes on these pages as you can, write, scribble, underline, highlight, and take a picture with your phone if you must. This list must be the things you are passionate about. Let me help you understand what I mean. These things that you are passionate about are the things that drive you to achieve the goals you want to achieve. It could mean that you want to achieve a new house, a financial peak, have a family, a business, anything. You need to complete this list with what's personal to you.

What are you passionately connected to? What drives you? Is it money? Success? Do you love what you do? Are you motivated to have a family? Are you always aiming higher towards a greater goal? Or do you like new challenges in life?

Make your list here:

....

....

....

Now, is this list inspiring you to achieve more? To put down this book and go do something positive?

Don't put this book down just yet, though! There's more to come. I want you to take a close look at all those things that you are passionately connected to, that drives you to achieve the goals you have set up; and to think deeply about them.

Now, what would happen if I were to come to you and say this: "You see this list? I'm going to take away all of those things from you!"

How would you feel? In fact, how would you feel if I were to take away even one of them? Or prevented you from doing just one of them?

Yes, you'd be upset, disappointed, angry, hurt, frustrated. Basically, you wouldn't be happy.

I know this because I ask everyone in my sessions about this, and those are the most common responses.

Now, don't think that life can't come over and bitch-slap you! It can, it probably has and it's probably priming itself up for another comeback! You've got to be prepared. You've got to be like a **peak performer** who knows how to play this game well. This is how successful people succeed when things don't go as planned. This will help you continuously get new business. Now there's a reason why I wanted you to list those things that you are passionate about, because they are important to you. In order for any of us to do those things that we are passionate about, that drives us, we must be taking action and do the work that is necessary so that we can afford both financially and in the amount of time, to be able to enjoy these things.

"I hated every minute of training, but I said, 'Don't quit. Suffer now and live the rest of your life as a champion."
~Muhammad Ali

Based on that, I'm going to take you into another exercise. Yes, this book is very practical and you should look forward to more exercises in the book. I don't want you to just read. I want you to be involved. This is how I learn and this is how you'd experience reading a book on a whole new level.

Why do I need to go to my job every day? Ask yourself that question and think about possible answers before reading any further. By answers, I don't mean 'money'.

Ask yourself more specifically, "What in my personal life makes me go to work every day?"

Is it because you have a family? You have expenses? Loans? Is it difficult to get another job? Or even at the same salary level? Could it be because of the type of management you have?

Make your list here:

....

....

....

You can't climb the ladder of success with your hands in your pockets. Remember, anyone can be cool, but awesomeness takes practice.

Look at your reasons above of what makes you go to work every day. You have responsibilities. You have a life and a certain lifestyle you must maintain. Without your job, wouldn't you agree that you'd face greater challenges in living life?

Connecting the things you are passionate about in the first exercise, take a closer look and you'll notice you need these reasons you just wrote, to get up and go to work every day. If you didn't have things that you wanted to achieve, if you didn't have those goals, if you didn't have those things that drive you in life that you are passionate about, how would you even enjoy anything that you do? We need to remember that other than responsibilities or push factors that make us go to work, there are also pull factors. These are the factors we enjoy about our jobs that help us enjoy the things we are passionate about and want to achieve. By being grateful for what's going on right at our workplace is a major step forward to enjoying our life overall.

Conversely, if we don't enjoy anything about our jobs, we won't be happy for most of the week because that's where we spend most of our time. If we're not happy most of the time, we are less inclined to be passionate about anything, or have anything that drives us. This is why so many people are unhappy at work and achieve little in life. It is also why there are others who look at the positives, have and achieve goals, enjoy things they are passionate about and are happier overall.

This is why effective communication is important in the workplace and with all your relationships. We can't get to that point without knowing how to communicate with others effectively. The better you are with people, and the better you can influence others, will help you along the way, mentally and emotionally. I want to start talking about how we can work with other people at a better level. How we can use the workplace for instance, and find things about our job that we enjoy, which would help us look forward to getting up to go to work every day? We first need to understand other people. How are other people different from us?

PEOPLE VS. OURSELVES

In order to be a success, we need to acknowledge that we are dependent on others, like it or not. There is no self-made billionaire without the help of others. Again, they couldn't make their riches if it had no one to pay them, right?

There's an interesting DVD that you can find online of a speech done by marriage counsellor and pastor, Mark called "A Tale of Two Brains" from his online programme *Laugh Your Way to a Better Marriage* (www.markgungor. com). I highly recommend you listen to his series and watch that video. He speaks of the differences between men and women and how they think differently from each other. He even goes on to describe how differently our brains are wired and how it affects the way in which we communicate with each other. Simply put, he says that men can think and do one thing at a time, whilst women are capable of thinking and doing many things at once.

Because of this, it affects how we all understand each other, process information, communicate and live as human beings dependent on one another.

Before we get into communication on a deeper level, I want you to recognise your own strengths and weaknesses. We are going to do some introspection. When was the last time you sat down, and wrote this down? Well, I want you to take a few minutes and do so now. But, let's categorise them into two areas; work life and personal life. What in your job are you really good at, and what in your personal life are you really good at? Also, let's put the areas where you believe you need to improve (weaknesses).

Strengths (work life e.g., sales, management, process, administration):

....
....

Strengths (personal life e.g. cooking, child care, dancing, painting):

....
....

Weakness (work life e.g., taking orders, remembering tasks, time management):

....
....

Weakness (personal life e.g., driving, swimming, whistling):

....

....

All done? You should feel a sense of accomplishment about all of your strengths. Focus on those. Be thankful that you have all those skills and abilities. Use that motivation as fuel in strengthening your weaker areas.

A **peak performer** always recognises his/her strengths and tries to develop his/her weaknesses. You are already a **peak performer** in many areas and you can achieve so much more.

> *Life is 10% what happens to you*
> *and 90% how you react to it.*
> **~Charles R. Swindoll**

I encourage attendees in my training courses to do these very exercises every single time. Most of the time, to my surprise, these people either haven't done exercises like these since they left school, or have never done it at all! This is why this book will be highly interactive. This is why, I am going slowly into techniques, which will be useful to your success in new business development at such a simple pace. We have started, we have started small.

This chapter mainly focuses on ourselves, our minds and what we need to do to become the people we want to be.

An experience I always go through which in no way is unique is, people's attitudes towards their jobs. I am there to empower and change lives of staff for companies, yet I always get complaints from them about the quality of their work conditions, decisions management makes, and there is no appreciation for the jobs they have. Granted there are companies that treat their staff unfairly and I understand that, but as people, we need to stop focusing on problems and start being solution finders and action takers.

Ask yourself this question now, "Do I love my job?"

If you love your job, or if you hate your job, there's got to be things that goes well wherever you work. Write down for yourself, what are the things that _you do like_ about your job. Now these things can either be because of the people you work with, how close you live from the office, how much money you make, if you have a good management team, if you're good at what you do. Think about all the things, even the little reasons about your job that you like.

I like my job:

....

....

....

....

....

Take a look back at what you've written above. How does that make you feel? Do you feel grateful for what you have right now? If not grateful, at least a bit better about it?

The purpose of making you list the reasons that are personal to you on why you enjoy your job is to remind you that these are the things that you've got going for you. The good things. The things that are valuable and very important in your work that gives you fulfilment.

THE CONCEPT OF MONEY
AND YOUR MIND

I want you to think on an even greater personal level. This next exercise that I want you to take note of, is only for you. This is about you. You should only share this if you want to. These notes are for you. I'm sure if you were to read this book again in five years you'd be amazed by the progress you have made.

Take two minutes and fill out the below table. This is your monthly budget. This is your breakdown of your income and expenses. This is not accounting at its most complicated level, but just a generalised breakdown of your finances. Share as many details you can to make this exercise worthwhile. I would be revisiting this as well as the other exercises you did earlier.

Look at the table below. Your task is to minus all your expenses from your main salary that hits your bank account after it is taxed (unless you pay your own taxes, then deduct it from your income). I have left some spaces without any information so you can include some of your other monthly commitments.

Salary (After Taxes)	-------------------------
Savings (Do not touch)	-------------------------
Rent	-------------------------
Groceries	-------------------------
Loans	-------------------------
Travel/gas	-------------------------
Utilities	-------------------------
----------------------	-------------------------
----------------------	-------------------------
----------------------	-------------------------
----------------------	-------------------------
Net (Surplus+/Deficit-)	

Your financial audit on yourself is now complete. Take a look at your final figure. Are you happy about it? Do you want to change it? Do you want that final figure to be in a surplus/ or greater surplus? Of course! Every company I work with, their staff tells me that they want that final figure to be in surplus and to increase it significantly because they have too many expenses.

In order to get yourself out of debt, I recommend two books that you should consider: *The Richest Man in Babylon* by George S. Clayson and *Rich Dad, Poor Dad* by Robert Kiyosaki. These are the best building blocks to start building the life you deserve, financially.

The table you filled out represents your life. I want you to see how this is similar to the first two exercises in this chapter about the things we are passionate about and why is it important for us to get up and go to work every day, no matter what we do or where we are. What if we were to take that same formula, and apply it to your company, or the company you work for? You may be the owner, a manager, a sales person there, but have you ever sat down and thought about your company as a living, breathing person? With responsibilities and every day commitments? I'm going to use that same formula in the table above and show you a simple concept with fictitious figures for easy understanding of the flow of the exercise. Please note the importance of understanding the flow and not the actual numbers. I am making this as simple as possible so even if you're under the age of 12 and you are reading this book, you'd understand this concept fully.

Monthly Sales	$500,000
Less Purchase of goods for resale	($350,000)
Gross Profit	$150,000
Less: Admin, Selling & General Exps:	
Accounting	($2,000)
Insurance	($10,000)
Interest on Loans	($5,000)
Maintenance and repairs	($5,000)
Motor vehicle	($15,000)
Rent	($10,000)
Salaries and bonuses	($60,000)
Taxes – Corporate	($30,000)
Travel	($3,000)
Utilities	($5,000)
Net Profit	$5,000

Suppose a company is really making that little. It's possible that they may be struggling for some time. However, the possibility exists where, the potential is there for such to take place!

If the profit figure above is that low, then the company may consider cutting cost and one of the first expense the company may consider cutting is salaries and bonuses.

If you were the owner of that company, wouldn't you feel the same way you did, when you had done the previous exercise on your personal finance? Wouldn't you feel as if there is something you need to do in order to change that outcome? Make it better?

Of course you would! This is why some company owners and managers feel pressured and frustrate employees to do tasks. This is why employees feel pressured to work and feel as if all their work goes in vain, without recognition or compensation. There is an obvious lack of communication. There is a gap because this information is not always available to everyone in a company.

In his best-selling book *The 7 Habits of Highly Effective People* by Stephen Covey started off by saying 'begin with the end in mind'.

Now, what if the company in the diagram faces a really slow month, or couple of months. Then their bottom line profits after all expenses would be even smaller! If that were to happen, what do you think would be the first thing you'd want to cut out from your expenses list if you had owned that company? Yes, salaries. This is why so many job losses have taken place in 2015 and 2016 with the low price of oil. Companies couldn't afford to keep people. Some tried keeping staff and eventually couldn't afford to do so anymore.

However, it is easy to see why these situations appear. Why people act the way they do when they see a company just made a million dollars for instance. Especially staff! But they have a right to do so! Simply, they don't know. Not only that, they don't know, that they don't know! All they see is the top figure.

We need to remember the things that drives us and what we are passionate about. Now, if we work better, smarter, harder and communicate at the best level with others, we would enjoy our jobs. When we enjoy what we do, we are more inclined to look forward to getting up and going to work every day. When we look forward to getting up and going to work every day, we are happier people. This trickles down to us achieving our goals and doing the things we are passionate about. Even developing our strengths and weaknesses. One thing leads or is connected to another. If we do not perform at what we do, how would we be able to enjoy the things we want to enjoy?

Compensation depends on performance and as such, performance is rewarded, financially, and/or in a motivational form. This in turn gives us the ability to afford a certain lifestyle or, the lifestyle we'd want. If we perform, get compensated for that performance and can afford to fulfil our goals and do the things that we are passionate about that drives us, then we would all live a happy and successful life. But, *success comes in after we put in the work*. Thus, work hard, do your best, communicate better with people, build long lasting relationships, and the rewards will come to you.

> *"Good, better, best. Never let it rest.*
> *'Till your good is better and your*
> *better is best"*
>
> **~St. Jerome**

Basically, when my company makes money, I make money. When I make money, I can afford to do the things I want to do and achieve. When I can afford to do the things I want and want to achieve, I am happy. When you're in sales, you have to think like a business owner, because you get rewarded according to the amount of effort you put within the time you work.

This is why I am focusing on communication in this book. The effective process of selling and communication and how beneficial it is to get your message across, clearly and precisely, with rewarding results in the end!

SELLING YOURSELF

I want you to be a success. I want you to learn how to control your finances, make more money, influence more people positively and help others achieve their goals. As the saying goes, what goes around, comes around.

Firstly, you need to focus on selling yourself as a person before you do anything. As the human race evolves into incredibly talented people with brilliant minds, to be successful, others need to see you working towards that success. Other people need to feel that positive vibes emanating from your soul and in order to do this, you need to communicate value to them. Verbally and non-verbally.

High performers don't wait for life to challenge them, they challenge themselves. They think beyond their current capabilities, to push themselves beyond their current self, above their abilities to their goals! By thinking like a **peak performer**, the possibilities for exponential growth as a person is endless.

Remember, the success mind-set is not just a matter of thinking like a successful person. It is an attitude. An attitude that makes up one's character. If you can accomplish developing an 'attitude of success', trust me, everything will work for you. Look at this story of a woman I'm going to tell you about. She had a problem, and reached out to Zig Ziglar for help. Have a look at this experience he once had and shared with one of his audiences in his talks.

This woman (let's call her Jane), was an unhappy person. Her frustration and unhappiness was apparent by her demeanour. She opened up when she went for help at one of his offices. But she entered with such force, that all her emotions just came flowing out of her. She almost started crying and said, *"I'm so glad to see you! I've got this horrible job. I hate it. I have everything about it. I hate everybody there."*

She was filled with so much negativity, yet she asked if he can help her. Mind you, this was just before he had to go to a meeting so he only had about 10 minutes. He stated in that speech that, he doesn't do any counselling, but talks to a lot of people who do. One thing that he noticed over the years is that many people, who go to counselling, are not necessarily looking for a solution. Amazing isn't it. Why would people do this? In fact, if I needed counselling, I thought I'd be looking for a solution.

He said he also couldn't understand it for a long time. Why would people bring a problem if they don't want to solve it? He discovered that people want to talk about it with everyone. They want to tell their story because they have people's attention. If you found the solution and in fact solved the problem, they can't tell you the problem again. They want the attention that goes with the problem! Every company has that kind of person, someone who wants attention through complaining.

He looked at her and said in a simple, easy-going way, *"I hear you and I think your problem is about to get worse."*

She said, *"What do you mean?"*

He replied, "I believe they're going to fire you!"

She was stunned, taken aback, in shock. *"Fire me! Why would they want to fire me?"*

Have you ever noticed that people who are the problem never notice that they are?

He went on to answer her by saying, *"Ma'am, I don't think there's a company big enough to contain such poison in one spot."*

Have you ever noticed when someone is about to lose something that they have been complaining about, in that moment, it increases in value? It was at that moment her tone changed as she asked, "Well, what can I do?" At this point she was open to suggestions.

Through a back and forth session in getting her convinced that his technique would give her amazing results, he finally convinced her to do the following tasks below. Here are the actions he made her take:

1. Write down and make a list of everything you like about your job 'I like my job because…' (she had over 20 things including her own parking spot, corner office, company paid trainings, and she was making a good salary).
2. Change the word 'like' to 'love' and repeat reading that list every morning when you wake up, and

before bed at night, in front of the mirror (from the first night she slept better).

3. Make it a daily habit and add more to the list (you can make or break a habit if you follow rule 21. This means that it can be done in 21 days). Once it becomes a habit, it would be the same as brushing your teeth. You do it every day as part of your routine.

A couple weeks later, they met and her approach was completely different. She came up to him with one of the biggest smiles he had seen. He asked, "How you're doing?"

Her response was so inspiring by saying, "I'm wonderful, and everything is well."

You see, she had developed a success mind-set through making a conscious decision in changing herself. She had been exposed to negativity all her life with her family telling her she wouldn't amount to much and her spouse doing the same. But she was able to change that despite all that she had gone through, all her life. Imagine my mentor, the late and great Zig Ziglar, having that experience and can share it with us so we won't make the same mistakes. You can do the same! You have the ability to be that **peak performer** with that success mind-set.

THE SUCCESS CYCLE BY
ANTHONY ROBBINS

"Start where you are. Use what you have.

Do what you can."

~Arthur Ashe

Anthony Robbins is one of the most influential persons in this world that I learn from. He is an American motivational speaker, personal finance instructor, and self-help author. He became well known from his infomercials and self-help books: *Unlimited Power, Unleash the Power Within* and *Awaken the Giant Within*.

He has a formula called 'The Success Cycle' that he uses in his seminars. I have personally followed this cycle to significantly improve my life and it has given me the ability to always seek out and try new things to achieve success. It is one of my mostly used motivational methods, whenever I have important decisions to make.

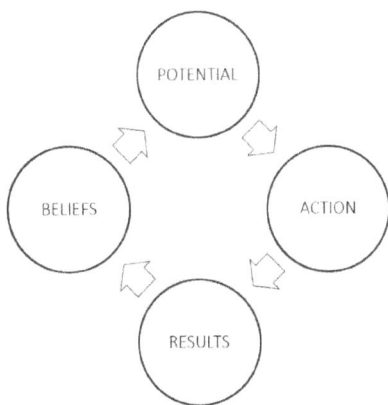

Tony goes on to explain that this cycle shows the reasons why the rich get richer and the poor get poorer.

He also makes it clear that being rich, does not necessarily refer to money. It could be happiness or fulfilment. Have you ever noticed that happy people tend to always be happy or get happier and depressed people always gets depressed or angry?

This demonstrates why that is so. Through the power of momentum.

Look at the first circle to the top. What is the amount of Potential that a person has within them? It's unlimited right? If a person like you has an unlimited amount of potential then that should mean you are capable of accomplishing anything you put your mind to. Let's think about the story of Clint I shared at the beginning of this chapter. If we were to take some of the potential or even a little pinch of it and put it into action as the second circle, we would see results as in the third circle right? Look at how many times Clint tapped into potential and took action.

Based on the action/s that you take and the results you are seeing, wouldn't your brain or subconscious tell you, 'Hey, this is a good idea, it's working' and you change your belief on how difficult you thought the task initially was by the time you got to the fourth circle? Now, if your belief has changed wouldn't you want to tap into more potential and take greater action and see even greater results than before? That's why he was able to continue pushing himself by taking action on many new business ideas. Wouldn't *you* believe in yourself even more and tap into more potential if you experienced the same?

This is how happy people get happier. This is how successful people achieve greater success. This is how self-confidence is built. Taking action is very important in succeeding at anything. Mere positive thinking alone won't work! Action also distracts the mind from over-thinking and worrying about 'what-if's' which helps in achieving positive results.

This also works in the reverse. Which is why sad people get depressed or angry, poor people get poorer etc. If you have unlimited potential and you think something won't work, you won't tap into that potential. Thus, you'd take little half-hearted or no action, see shitty results and your mind would ask you 'why did you even bother to try?' You convince yourself that it wasn't going to work and so repeat the cycle with less or no effort and stay in a depressed state or even worse, give up!

Which direction are you going to choose to succeed?

"Failure will never overtake me if my determination to succeed is strong enough."

~Og Mandino

Ever since I started following his teachings, this cycle made the biggest impact on my life. It has given me new ways to observe different situations, take on new challenges and look forward to things in the future. Writing these words right now is part of taking action. I know that when I'm done writing this book, I'd see positive results which would only enhance my belief in my own capabilities. By the time you are finished reading this book, you too would see positive results just from the actions you are taking. You can do the same thing! You need to draw that cycle out on a piece of paper and stick it up on your bathroom mirror, bedroom mirror, refrigerator and anywhere it can be right in front of your face! By seeing it continuously, you'd always ask yourself, "What action am I going to take today to achieve my goals?"

Henry Ford once said, "Whether you think you can, or you can't you're right". That statement is just a few words, yet it fully explains Tony Robbins' Success cycle! If you think you can, your chances of tapping into additional potential is greater than if you think you cannot. Which in turn affects your results and beliefs!

I'd like you to think about the next goal you want to achieve. Ask yourself these questions below and as you progress, write down everything that happens and track your progress. I expect you to do the first two items now.

i.   How can I tap into my potential? What does it mean? Is this related to the section on my passion and interests? What am I good at that I can apply to achieving this goal/milestone (strengths)?

....
....
....
....

ii.   What actions do I need to take to fulfil that potential? What do I need to do, step-by-step?

....
....
....
....

iii. Results. Let's assume, it's related to the financial breakdown. You could state that your financial audit (statement) is a reflection on your actions. If the financial statement is zero that means the actions taken have not been useful. Which means, you need to re-think the actions to re-tap into your potential.

....
....
....
....

iv.   What beliefs can you reaffirm in yourself after a
        small taste of success? What can you repeat in this
        cycle?

....

....

....

....

A perfect example would be the story of Roger Bannister, a man born on 23 March 1929, who was a former English middle-distance athlete, physician and academic, who ran the first sub-four-minute mile. After his relative failure at the 1952 Olympics, Bannister spent two months deciding whether to give up running. He set himself on a new goal: to be the first man to run a mile in under four minutes. Accordingly, he intensified his training and did hard intervals.

On 2 May 1953, he made an attempt on the British record at Oxford. Paced by Chris Chataway, Bannister ran 4:03.6, shattering Wooderson's 1945 standard. Based on that result Bannister said, "This race made me realise that the four-minute mile was not out of reach".

The claim that a four-minute mile was once thought to be impossible by *informed* observers was and is a widely propagated myth created by sportswriters and debunked by Bannister himself in his memoir, *The Four Minute Mile* (1955). The reason the myth took hold was that four minutes was a round number which was slightly better (1.4 seconds) than the world record for nine years, longer than it probably otherwise would have been because of the effect of the World War II in interrupting athletic progress in the combatant countries. The Swedish runners Gunder Hägg and Arne Andersson, in a series of head-to-head races in the period 1942-45, had already lowered the world mile record by five seconds to the pre-Bannister record.

On 6 May 1954, Bannister ran the four-minute mile in three minutes and 59.4seconds. But how did he do it? Practice? Yes that contributed to it, but deep down was something greater than physical practice. It was mental. Bannister tapped into untapped potential by seeing himself breaking that record. He did it so many times during his practice that he believed it. What he believed of himself came to pass when he broke that record. While running, his knowledge of pace deserted him. He had heard over the cheering someone say, "relax" which made him thought that if the speed was wrong as he was already into a minute of the race, why worry. He said that he listened and became so relaxed it felt as if his mind was detached from his body.

On the last lap, he only had 59 seconds to achieve the four minute mark, he picked up his pace, his mind took over and in his words he said, "My mind raced well ahead of my body, and drew me compellingly forward". When he crossed the finish line, he knew he had done it, before he heard about it. In the last 50 years the four-minute mile record has been lowered by almost 17 seconds!

It always seems impossible until it's done! As Robin Sharma nicely puts it, "The way we do small things determines the way we do everything".

Peak performers demand more of themselves and challenge themselves all the time! He was the high achiever! He was a success because of how he conditioned himself in his mind! Through physical and mental practice! People are not born experts, they become experts through the things they do. What they do, they turn into habits. You are a result today of the habits you have created. You will be the person you want to become by the actions you take today and turn into habits!

This is how the success cycle works!

INSPIRING INTENTIONS

You don't have to be great to start, but you have to start to be great. What a wonderful philosophy to start any day! How inspiring are those few words if you were to think about them a few minutes before you do any great task?

In order to communicate effectively with others and be a success in sales, in business or in life, you need to be inspired before you inspire others.

Your intentions does not have to be associated with your current world or life. What I mean by this is, that an intention you set for yourself acts as a goal or an action plan. Something or someone you want to become. You are at your current level of success in your career, or position in life based on the intentions you had set for yourself in the past. If you are not yet where you'd like to be, you can set for yourself new intentions, new goals and change the course of your life to achieve the things you'd like to achieve or become the person you'd like to become. Your past does not have to dictate the intentions you set for yourself from today. The past is the past.

In fact, your intention can be disassociated from your current identity. Remember, the intention you set for yourself, is to become the person you'd like to be! So no matter where you are now, no matter what you do, no matter how much money you have or do not have, you can set the course of your life from today! But it is up to you to first decide, and then commit. The latter is the hardest part because many people decide to change but old habits die hard and they fail to commit. That's why marriages fail, businesses don't thrive for as long as it has potential to, why people jump from job-to-job.

Right now I want you to complete the following exercise. Take a couple of minutes, to make a list of the top 10 things you intend to do to become the person you want to become. If you can't get 10, I recommend at least five.

I intend to:

1. ....
    ....
2. ....
    ....
3. ....
    ....
4. ....
    ....
5. ....
    ....
6. ....
    ....
7. ....
    ....
8. ....
    ....
9. ....
    ....
10. ....
    ....

This is the reason why successful people do what failures won't. Look at Richard Branson, Mark Cuban, Daymond John, Mark Zuckerberg, Bill Gates, Steve Jobs, Mark Benoiff, Andy Harrington, Oprah, Elon Musk and all the success stories of many other amazing people you'd be reading about later on in this book. What do they all have in common? They all started with an intention, a vision, and a goal, made their minds up that they are going to do great things and stuck to it no matter what challenges they faced! They committed themselves to becoming persons of value after setting their intentions to change the world despite their position in life at the time they made that decision.

SUMMARY

- Remember the things you are passionately connected to and how you'd feel if you were to lose it. Be grateful for those opportunities and all you have in your life.
- Remember the reasons why you do enjoy your work and every day repeat those reasons saying "I love my work because."
- Remember the reasons why you get up every morning to go to work.
- Periodically do a strengths and weakness analysis on yourself. This will help you track your progress.
- Follow Anthony Robbins' Success Cycle and every day ask yourself, "What potential can I tap into today?"
- Always ask yourself how you intend to take action to get the results you want whenever you tap into your potential.
- Set intentions that inspire you every day.

Always remember, gratitude is the key to a great life. At any moment some things are going well, while others are not going as we would choose. Being grateful for the blessings of life, including the life lessons that come from our setbacks, sets your mind for positive thinking and for enjoying a great life.

Remember, your present situation is not your final destination. The best is yet to come.

CHAPTER 2

SALES vs SELLING

"Self-Leadership is daily discipline."
~Todd Duncan

Have you ever heard the saying, "Nothing happens until somebody sells something?" This has been a well-known saying in the industry for decades. It has never changed, and I don't think that it will; but it should!

The current business environment and the use of technology have helped many new businesses spring up out of nowhere and become successful. However, I must state that in reference to the name of this chapter, *sales* and *selling* are two different things. Saying that nothing happens until somebody sells something, is absurd, because if that were true, then we'd all sit at home, make sales, get fat and be merry! Let me start by explaining the differences. A sale is the last step in the chain of commerce. This is where cash is exchanged for the product or service. What this book will focus on, would be the strategies surrounding 'how to get more sales'. In other words, "selling", and the communication techniques behind them all.

In this modern age of technology, the terminologies of 'sales' and 'selling' are being replaced by social marketing. Let me be straight with you. First of all, marketing is not selling. Marketing is not sales. Marketing is the tool or process that brings sales opportunities to you or your business.

> *"Marketing is what makes the phone ring.*
> *Selling is what you do when you answer."*

In order to make your business a success in generating revenue, you must understand a customer's journey in their decision making process. An ad in the newspaper, social media, television, digital screen does not capture that information. Human contact does! No one ever makes purchases by coming to you and saying, "Here's my credit card, let me know when you're done". There needs to be communication between the seller or company and the customer or buyer.

What makes this book special is that we would be looking closely at the communication techniques that give you total control of any conversation while making your customer or any listener, feel as if they are entirely in control. They would feel super important. In turn, feel so comfortable with you, that they'd want to do business with only you!

What you'll learn in this book as well, is the art of commitment. Many times people perceive selling to be bothersome by trying to push as much sales and get lots of major commitments from customers, yet, because of that attitude, they fail to achieve targets and make as much money as they should be making. It is not about pushing a sale so aggressively that you'd get to a close, but rather through commitments along the way. What I mean by this is that we need to work with a customer and get them comfortable with what we're saying from the start of the conversation. They need to agree with all our points along the way. They need to be on our side but also feel comfortable knowing that we are also on their side.

Let me share an interesting story with you about my friend Robert. Robert Rolih is the *European Public Speaker of the Year 2015* (awarded by London's Professional Speakers Academy). At his seminars he shares what the financial industry doesn't want us to know about investing. Robert shared with me a brief story on how he got started in sales and how he used selling techniques and communication to effectively work with others to achieve success. However, it was not always success when he had just started. Here's the story as told by him:

> *"Adrian, quickly I will tell you that firstly, I grew up poor in a backwater village in a small country but I became a successful entrepreneur and started to cooperate with people like Brian Tracy and Chet Holmes. I lost a **lot of** money because I trusted financial advisers and made huge mistakes but I grew and learned from those mistakes and invested sevenyears and more than $100,000.00 in my financial education. But it wasn't just that.*

> *When I was a student, I started my first company in a student dorm with just a phone and a computer. At the time, my parents were really poor and didn't have money to help me. So I basically started from zero. No connections, nothing. So back then, I was selling web design services which at the time was not as popular as it is today. I was basically creating different web pages for businesses and selling my services one-to-one in meetings. I'd usually make cold calls and get in touch with potential clients where I'd try to arrange meetings of which I'd go to and sell my services. However, at the time, I knew nothing about selling. I didn't even know it was a 'thing' with a process. Although I thought I was good at getting business, reality was totally different.*

Let's say, I'd be going to meetings from those phone calls, I'd basically go to about ten meetings and out of those ten meetings I'd probably get business from zero to one client out of those meetings! These were my results!

Then everything started to really bother me. I had bills to pay as a student, and because of not getting those results I began to worry. Then something very interesting happened.

I used to read books by Brian Tracey on leadership and business strategy, but never the ones about selling. But one day on my book shelf, I noticed one of his books called 'Advanced Selling Strategies'. I said to myself, maybe there would be a solution in this for me. I started to read this book and it was like,, "Wow" because up until that moment, I thought that selling is an art. You know, go to the meeting and talk with the client in a certain way and so on! The viewpoint in the book was totally different because it taught me that selling is not an art, but a science. That every sale has about four distinctive phases, and one needs to go through these stages or phases in order to make a sale. This information really hit me by surprise because I really didn't know that there were phases one must go through. I learnt about how to build trust and identify needs, present your product or service and close the sale.

These things were new for me and it brought structure in my meetings. When I started to implement these techniques, I began to read more books on the topic and attend more seminars. This made me really good at selling. In the years that followed, having started getting one out of ten meetings, I was now closing on average eight out of ten people I met with! From that, I was able to make a lot of money and gain new customers taking the company to one of the most profitable web design company in our country.

Since then I was able to move my career forward into teaching people about the things the financial industry does not want us to know because I also realised that web design would have become a commodity and did not want to be left behind. The success I built from that start now takes me all over, because of the principles I use all the time from selling. It helps me communicate with everyone.

Now the reason why I wanted you to know Robert's story is because it shows you how simple techniques used effectively can take one from a position of uncertainty to a position of success by gaining little commitments from clients using the effective communication techniques found in selling. You will learn more about this in detail as you continue to read on in this book.

Robert Rolih is the European Public Speaker of the Year 2015 (awarded by London's Professional Speakers Academy), and an Amazon Bestselling author of *The Million Dollar Decision*.

At his seminars he shares what the financial industry doesn't want us to know about investing.

You can learn more about him at www.robertrolih.com

We would begin in this chapter to work on gaining those many commitments and agreements from customers. Commitments that would make them comfortable and feel as if they are in total control, build trust with you, and make them want to buy from you -rather than feel as if they're being sold to. Just as Robert showed us in his experience.

> *"Communication is not about*
> *speaking what we think,*
> *Communication is about ensuring*
> *others hear what we mean."*
> **~Simon Sinek**

Before we do this, let me share some history with you. There is a huge stigma attached to the "sales job". If we continue to believe this stigma, and not begin to change the attitudes towards the title, we will forever be in a position of uncertainty whenever we see job vacancies, for sales people. What I mean by this is, in doing sales, many people do not like to apply for such a job. Many people who do apply don't stay long in the job and a cycle is created which is why many companies are always hiring or looking for new salespeople to fill those positions.

Daniel Pink explains it best in his many talks. You should look him up and consider his book, *To Sell is Human*. Here's how I am going to explain it to you.

Back when the world was in its industrialisation era, there were many door-to-door salesmen. This is back in the 1950s and 60s. Now these salesmen were the masters of persuasion and very good at convincing people. However, what they sold weren't always quality products. They were able to convince people to buy from them but, the quality of the items were either sub-standard, or the after service sucked. In turn, the customers experienced buyer's remorse. For the many years or rather decades that happened, over time, people considered anyone who was a salesman to be sleazy, pushy, and dishonest individuals. Which is why today, whenever you hear about a salesman, or you even hear the word, one cringes in their stomach and you see for yourself, people reacting negatively!

Take for example insurance sales people. Now for developing countries I am not here to bash insurance sales, in fact, I endorse insurance. It is very important to be covered for any kind of disaster or illness or accident. It has and will continue to help millions of people around the world. But in developing countries, these salespeople are viewed as pushy, sleazy, dishonest and as a plain waste of time. Not because of the job or the product, but because of their approach! Would you believe that in this modern world, insurance salespeople still use an "ancient" approach to their prospective customers? They solidify the point that we should fear the salesman or receiving a call from a salesman!

I have had many branch/ agency managers from top insurance firms approach me to work with them but it just wasn't my passion. Because of my experience in sales and having many insurance sales people approach me, I realise that most of them have a standard script that they either are trained on or use out of habit. To you insurance salesperson reading this, and especially the one wondering why it is so hard to get proper meetings, in this modern world we live in, this script is not enticing customers to have a meeting with you anymore. Which is why you'd spend so many times cold-calling and not getting as many meetings as you deserve to!

Why do I say this? Here's the phone calls I've received. They generally went like this:

"Good morning, I'm trying to reach Adrian Havelock"

"Speaking."

"Hi Adrian/Mr. Havelock, my name is John Smight and I'm calling from the X Company. I'd like to meet with you to discuss some opportunities that I think would be beneficial to you."

My first thought after hearing that line is, 'Wait, what? You don't know me. You don't know what I'm in the middle of doing. You don't know who I am, so how can you be sure your opportunities are beneficial to me?'

Anything you say beyond that point will be trumped by the feeling I (Mr. Potential Customer) feel, after hearing your 'salesy' introduction. I usually just kindly inform them that I am not interested in anything at this time but wish them all the success in their sales.

This is the first reason why only some insurance sales people do really well, and the majority either barely break through or don't stay in the industry for too long. It is also another reason why the industry always advertise for new salespeople with 'great remuneration packages'.

I know that the industry has recently begun changing up those scripts but I am yet to receive a call with the new interesting script that really hooks my attention and respects my time! (No, that does not give you permission to be flooding my mobile with calls right now). But, do you understand why the general public looks at the job title with a bit of disgust? I will talk with you on this phone call script a little more later on in the chapter. You'd love the approach when you use it with real clients.

What makes this even more interesting is that we no longer live in the Industrialization era! We now live in the modern world of information technology! We live in the information age! In this era we live in, customers no longer need to depend on the salesman to educate them on the product or service. They no longer have to be influenced, and experience any buyer's remorse. They no longer need much of a salesman in most cases because they can buy online!

They can research everything they need online and decide from there if they need to buy! You're probably wondering, do we even need the salesman again? Yes! Developing countries and certain products and services in all countries still require human interaction and communication skills! The sales process needs to give the one who is selling the ability to bring value to the buyer! Not everyone makes decisions based on logical reasons and facts, many people need to feel an emotional connection, and only through communication, can that connection of value be made.

Do you see why it's important to connect with people to achieve success? Without it, the world would not move forward. All the existing and upcoming technological advancements won't fully replace our dependency on each other as a species to survive and to do business of course!

A 'NORMAL' JOB?

There are millions of surveys for many little things and many different areas. I remember a talk I once heard being delivered, that really stood out to me about jobs. As I recall, the speaker, Daniel Pink, stated that in a survey that was done, there was a calculation of the number of people in direct sales jobs to the rest of the working population. By direct sales jobs, it meant anyone who was in a position to generate sales through their efforts such as insurance sales people, car sales, retail sales, real estate, consulting etc. The rest of the working population was classed as 'normal' jobs that didn't require direct selling.

The results from the survey indicated that 1/10 of the population did direct selling, or one in ten people. But think for a second, do you agree with those numbers? Is it really one in ten persons who sell? To many, it seems relatively realistic and believable. I can see why many people would think this. In fact, if I thought about jobs I'd think, doctor, police officer, lawyer, technician, fireman, janitor, insurance sales person, cashier, and a business owner. Wait, that's 10 people! Just one of them is in a direct sales job! Or is it just one?

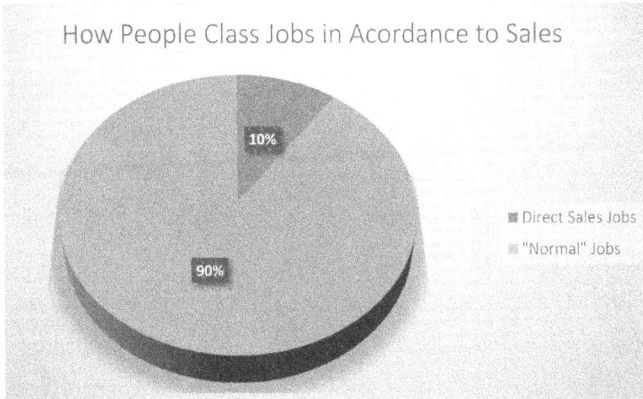

How People Class Jobs in Acordance to Sales

10%

90%

■ Direct Sales Jobs
■ "Normal" Jobs

Actually, we all sell!

But how? Here's the thing. When you go to an interview for a job, you have to sell the interviewer on why you would be a good fit for their company. You have to sell yourself! Another example, if you have a kid around the house and you just got them to pick up their toys, you had to sell them on the idea that picking up the toys is a good deed and if not done, would result in 'major' consequences. You had to convince them. Now, if you have to convince people every day to either do you a favour, or get something or help you with something, you just sold that person on that activity! That basically means you performed a non-sales sale!

That brings up a new question: how much time do you spend convincing others, or persuading them to give something of value, like their attention or time, or effort?

Well, seeing that I'm on a survey streak right now, I'd just go straight to the results! The average individual spends 40% of their time persuading others for something. Now picture this: you spend 40% of your time persuading others in a day, a week, a month, imagine how much money you'd be making if you knew that you have always been selling. Basically, the sales process is not too different from what you already do. It boils down to putting a process to what you've always done in persuading others, following it, and leading to an 'agreement' which is the 'close'.

PERSUADING ➡ CONVINCING ➡ PERSUADING ➡ CONVINCING ➡ AGREEMENT/ CLOSE

Usually in working with many people over the years the topic that comes up, out of this is, only a certain type of people are capable of being good in sales. That they need to have a certain personality. I believe that only a small percentage is true. Rarely this has to be the case because sales is something that anyone can do well once they put their minds to do it right. But what also makes successful companies and successful sales teams and individuals is the ability to overcome fear and objections (which I will deal with later on in this book).

Once you have the ability to do that and keep pushing forward, the rewards in life as a whole would be worth it. Set goals, and in this case, a sales target. Continuously push forward and pursue and you will succeed. Many people do not last in sales jobs because they do not want to work. They rather sit back and collect a salary at the end of the month. In sales, you get paid for the amount of effort you put in. Each month you can determine how much money you want to make.

THE PRINCIPLE OF TARGETING

Let's focus now on that effort. Let's talk about a principle which is very relevant to sales. This principle is the key to succeeding in this modern world of communication through all the different channels of communication. Without this principle being effectively used, for any one, getting new business would be an arduous and stressful task. But if used wisely, it can mean the world in your success. That is the 80/20 Principle that I learned from reading a really good book by Perry Marshall called *The 80/20 Sales and Marketing*. But just for the focus of this book, let me share a brief detail of how this works.

80/20

The 80/20 principle or rule, is something that we are all not aware of, yet is no stranger to us. It exists in everything that surrounds us. Simply put, for many events roughly 80% of the effects comes from 20% of the causes. That being said it is common to hear that 80% of your sales comes from 20% of your clients. 80% of the traffic is on 20% of the roads. In business, Marshall stated that 80% of your results comes from 20% of your efforts and 20% of your results comes from the other 80%. This rule applies to so many things in the world you'd be surprised as to how deep it goes and we do not notice it. After reading this and especially after reading his book, you'll begin to see that you'd notice the 80/20 in everything. For example, in a business you can measure the 80/20 in:

- Your sales team's performance: the top 20% brings in 80% of the business.
- Location of customers in your store:80% of them mostly spend time in 20% of the floor space.
- Product popularity: selling products adds up to 20% that brings in 80% of the money.

- Problem employees:20% of them creates 80% of the controversy.
- Reasons customers buy: 20% of the reasons are shared by 80% of the customers.
- Sources of customer traffic from online marketing: 80% of the customers comes from 20% of your target market.

There are so many more examples I can show you how the 80/20 principle can apply to anything in our lives.

Now that you have an idea of how the 80/20 works, let us start using this principle in the way we work. In the way we get new business and in the way we make money. Think of this, if you want to advertise something on a billboard, and that's the ONLY form of advertising you have at your disposal, would you place one thousand billboards in different residential areas or one billboard along a highway? Exactly, your thoughts are correct! One billboard on a highway will generate 80% customer viewing whereas one thousand billboards in residences would be only 20% customer viewing because 80% of the effort and money and resources went into the billboards, whereas, along the highway, 20% work was to set up the billboard where 80% of the viewership takes place. Take a look at this; if you want to make $100,000.00 in your business, would you try to get 20 companies to buy $5,000.00 worth in products and services from you or would you try to work with five companies who'd spend $20,000.00 each?

Yes, we want those five companies. It sounds easier to work with the top five companies there, but remember, when getting customers/clients like that, it takes more effort. Spend 80% of your time trying to get that top 20% of quality clients continuously, and spend 20% of your time maintaining or servicing them. This way it is more focused.

THE PERFECT PROSPECTING PLANNER (PPP)

The PPP as I would call it, is the process by which 'on the field' sales people would get new customers. If you own or work in retail business then that would not necessarily require having to find new clients, thus the PPP would not necessarily be as useful. That's because your sales would be dependent on the conversions you make from customers who call or enter your establishment or purchase from online.

If your products or services depends on having to reach out to new companies or customers, you'd find this very useful. At the end of the day, communication takes place and you begin at this point in dealing with people.

I've realised that online marketing techniques to drive sales is becoming very popular especially in developed countries. This is where you see an ad online via a page or a video and it says to "click here" or "enter your e-mail address for some free promotion" and so on. We even fall for some of these strategies by giving our information and our e-mail inbox is either flooded with good content or promotional e-mails.

I am not writing this book to give you techniques on how to achieve that. There are many resources online that shows you how to get that done successfully. This book, and in particular this chapter, focuses on the one to one direct communication lines. How do we get in touch with the right people? How do we do that in a developing country? How do we get onto the right people in companies we'd want to enter?

Before we even begin to go out and find new customers there are some ground rules. Firstly, not all sales involves actively seeking out new buyers. Some sales comes from retail establishments, online sales, and personal services. There are different approaches involved in getting new buyers. But once you have that potential customer, the sales process remains generally the same until you close the sale.

What about those ground rules? Well, prospecting is the most important activity when selling because the single largest investment is always earmarked for attracting first time customers.

We need to know firstly, what are we selling?

As a professional, you need to know what you are selling. This goes beyond the product/service. It also involves its application and uses.

We also need to understand our target market. What are the sectors of the economy, what types of companies or persons would be in the market to buy our products or services?

Who are the individuals in the target market that would be responsible for making the decisions to buy?

If it's companies, where in the companies would you have to target or position your sales?

Finally, and most importantly, who are your competitors and what are their strengths and weaknesses?

Now that we have a better understanding of what we are selling, we need to write it down. Use the table below and include the information. Try to get as much information as possible. If you don't have enough space available, get a piece of paper and continue it, then stick it to this page.

What am I selling?	Answers
Type of Products and Services	
Target Market	
Who are the individuals that are important?	
Where in the companies (if different from above)?	
Competitors and their strengths and weaknesses	

If you were doing this exercise and realise that some of the information you are writing in the different categories are the same, that's fine. Depending on what you are selling or what industry you're in, your answers may over-lap into other categories. Great! Now that you have all of this information about yourself, your next task would be to use it wisely. Which takes us to the next rule of the PPP:

1. Getting the Information

This rule is the first part of your ability to find that perfect 80/20 customer. That 20% customer who will give you 80% of the business or income you make. Getting the information is the process of acquiring as much contact information and overall understanding about the companies/individuals you'd like to sell to. Once you have all the right contact information, you can then begin reaching out to them.

Before you read on, think for a moment and decide, where's the first place I'd go in order to get information about companies or people. Yep, online!

Now that you've done that, look at the many different resources you may have at your disposal that you can use to fully inform and educate yourself with the knowledge of, and about that potential customer, in order to win business and be successful.

We can use:

A. The Internet.
B. Telephone directory.
C. Tailored mailing lists.
D. Business magazines such as *Who's Who Magazine*.
E. Existing databases.
F. Networking events.
G. Annual reports (printed or published in the media).
H. Local business links or government bodies.
I. Business associations' listings online.
J. Advertisements in the newspapers (these have contact information which makes it easy to build your own database as well).
K. Billboards.
L. Advertising on a company's trucks wherever their logo is located to advertise their business.
M. Referrals from friends and associates.

By using a combination of those resources, and there are more, you and equip yourself with as much knowledge about your potential customers. But it goes beyond contact information!

You also need to understand that if it's a company, what type of company. What do they do? What are their needs? Who are their suppliers?

Utilise social media, such as Facebook, LinkedIn, Twitter, Instagram and Google+. This gives you active information about their operations and a real inside look into their industry as well.

It is very important that you take notes. As many as possible. Which encourages me to emphasise that technology is very important. Your mobile phone is not just to make calls and post selfies and check or update Facebook and Twitter. It is a weapon. A *sales weapon*.

Look at the many things you can do with a mobile phone in today's world! You can:

- Snap vital contact information with your phone.
- Use barcode scanners for information or to take you to different links.
- Use augmented reality for the same.
- Compose and e-mail documents and attachments.
- Communicate with others real time anywhere in the world via video or audio.

- Open folders.
- You have an app for anything and everything!
- It's basically a computer in your hand because you can back up and retrieve information as well!

Now that you have a better understanding of how to go about getting information on persons and companies (also key persons in companies), your next task is to use those resources now and find information on five major companies or people you wish to target your products or services to. This should take you no more than 15-20 minutes with the use of a telephone directory, mobile phone, internet access etc. Bookmark this point and go ahead and start that now. Bookmark this line and stop reading for now. Take 10 minutes and do this exercise now.

2. Filtering the information

Well done on both exercises earlier. You now have a better understanding of what you are selling and you just successfully acquired information on some potential customers/clients. What are you going to do with that information now? Sell them? No.

As you have that information, we first need to know if all the information or persons or companies are relevant in the first place!

John Wanamaker, who was a United States merchant and religious, civic and political figure, was considered the father of modern advertising and a pioneer in marketing. He famously said, "Half of the money I spend on advertising is wasted, the trouble is, I don't know which half ." We need to know which half we are going to spend on.

Filtering the information is all about cleansing your list to make it as accurate as possible. You've got to make sure that your product or service can be utilised efficiently by the customer. Either directly or in their business. It makes no sense a pharmaceutical salesperson tries to approach a bistro owner to sell them (unless they have a pharmacy as an additional business. But you won't know that unless you did the exercises earlier now would you?).

This is the best time to apply the 80/20 principle that we discussed above!

This way, you'd be able to spend more time with better prospects. The law of probability states that the more time you spend with better prospects, the more sales you'll make. I would also go on further to state that you'd be better able to measure your return on investment in keeping with tracking your progress and success. Techniques all of which will help you build on your strengths and weaknesses. Your own key performance indicators (KPI).

Let's cleanse that list of the five major companies or people you'd like to target now. Take five minutes.

In order to sell anything, we basically have to start from the end and work our way back to the beginning. By doing the first three areas above you have successfully completed where you need to go in order to find the right people or companies. Remember, Stephen Covey said to 'begin with the end in mind'.

Sales is no longer a qualification process where you need to just identify the best prospects. It is more of a disqualification process, because the more junk you can eliminate before you spend money and effort, the better you'll be!

3. An Effective Contact Strategy

Now that we have the information on these companies and/or individuals, how do we go about reaching out to these people? Call them? Well, that's one way, but it doesn't always work out when we run to the phones as the first thing. That's 'cold-calling'. However, I believe in a strategy that's not so cold.

We first need to create awareness to these individuals about ourselves before we can pick up the phones and try to sell them or get meetings. I usually encourage staff and anyone I coach to use a 'warm-up strategy' before making any phone calls. I would also be encouraging you to do the very same as you read along as well. This book is interactive and in order to achieve success in winning new business, you must apply them in real time.

We are going to use mailshots or email marketing. Do Not Cold Call! Sometimes, I use WhatsApp (only if the individuals already knows who I am and I have already built a relationship with them).

The only time you are allowed to cold call anyone, is only if your job is strictly telemarketing. In this 21st Century of technology, even telemarketing is fading.

I personally believe that in order to do business with anyone especially for direct selling, face-to-face is very important!

These mailshots or e-mails are not to sell anything but to create interest. When you call, you do not sell any product or services but confirm if the information you sent interests them and if it does, book a meeting. That's it! Simple! Straightforward. If it does not interest them, next customer to call!

But in anything persuasive, there is a lot of science and psychology which is involved in everything you say, do or type. Let us deal with the design of your e-mail/letter. You must have the words clearly explaining yourself as well as it needs to be in a specific order. If that is not done, you would be less likely to seek any interest from any customer in wanting to meet you. But, presented the correct way, you can definitely book more meetings, more frequently.

Here's what you are trying to achieve from this point onwards:

- Effective letter/e-mail correspondence.
- A follow-up phone call that references the correspondence sent (it's not a cold call but a warm/first call).
- A meeting booked as a result of that call.

Remember the example of the insurance salesperson telephone call script earlier? That's a cold call. In my book, a call like that, no matter the industry you're in should be a 'no-no'.

Let's deal with the first step in the warm up strategy; an effective letter/e-mail correspondence.

There needs to be a specific structure to this e-mail. This structure is important. I will have an example later on for you to use but remember, each person, product or service would be different, so my example may not necessarily suit what you sell. Use it in your own words, use your personality in it. But keep the structure for effectiveness.

Contact Strategy Structure for E-mail/Letter

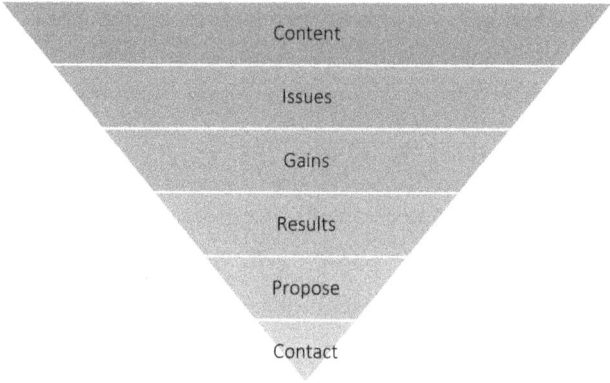

Look at the above table. Below each point is a next step to follow in designing your email structure.

Note: We cannot construct an effective letter or e-mail following this structure if we have not done proper research on the potential customer and made sure that we filtered them properly. This must be done first.

I want to get a customer interested in what I do and what I have to say. But before I start talking about myself I need to know more about the customer and use that information wisely. When I send this e-mail or letter to them, I want to be sure that they like what they see and so should you.

Please do not:

- Send long e-mails or letters, it won't be read.

- If it's an e-mail, do not type out the email from the left of your screen to the right. Use half of the text space and press enter/return to create a next line which shortens your lines. To the human eye, this is easier to read in comparison to typing full sentences from the left to the right of your screen.

- Do not sell any product or service.

- Do not use the word/s 'great opportunity' or 'benefit', It's too salesy.

- Speak about yourself but only in the context of being the contact person.

Now the structure is made up of six parts. Content – Issues – Gains – Results – Proposal – Contact.

That's the order or flow of your e-mail:

1. The first point (content) is to get their attention to read on.
2. The 'issues' is a point made about their industry from the research you would have done.
3. The gains are the main solutions that have helped those issues (as a customer I'm still interested in reading on).
4. The results can be an example (this is optional).
5. The proposal is a suggestion that you (customer) can benefit from the same/similar solutions.
6. The contact basically states that you would be contacting them soon.

No way am I going to leave it up to the customer to contact me if interested. I'd be leaving money on the table if I do that, because good customers can slip right through my fingers...

Now I want you to read over those points above. Do they make sense to you? The reason it's in that order is because I need to grab their attention, keep it and let them know I'll be making contact. Even if they forget that I would call them, when I do, they'll remember because it was the last thing I stated in the e-mail/letter.

Take a look at the example below. I want you to develop a letter/email of your own following the format and example as a guide:

Dear Mr./Mrs.

(Advanced acquired knowledge/ identify present issues.)

Did you know that for firms to reach $1 Million in revenue in two months will require a system that turns your raw materials into shelf placed products within three days?

(Broad overview of benefit.)

Similar companies have used a system that achieves that production rate while reducing expenses. One of the ways they've been able to achieve this is by online sales via credit card purchases and offering free delivery because of a moulding machine that immediately labels the products when produced and is also connected throughout the company so the marketing department can know real time what's the latest products!

(Show positive results of your product.)

XYZ Peppers Ltd., has told us they have been able to achieve such a feat. Here are some specific results they are presently experiencing:

- *28.7% Increase in revenue monthly.*
- *An overall increase in sales annually.*
- *Reduced advertising costs.*
- *Increased customer loyalty.*

(Suggest he/she can see similar results).

Would you like to experience similar results? I will follow-up with you on Wednesday to discuss in more detail.

Regards,
Adrian N. Havelock

Are you are you able to identify in the letter where the structure comes in? Also, can you tell that was an e-mail by the length of the sentences? Had I written it across the page, it would have seemed a lot longer to read by the human brain.

Now if you take a closer look at the structure, it's not broken up into exactly six categories. Some are combined into one statement or paragraph, another is left out. Practice a couple e-mail or letter formats and develop your own style but make sure you keep the flow.

Here's your task. Write an e-mail or letter using the flow described earlier. Make sure you give free content/information that would first hook the attention of the reader. Re-read it as if you're the customer and ask yourself, does this hook my interest? Ask yourself that question after every sentence, you'd know if you feel like reading further if you were to receive such a letter or e-mail.

Free information (for example, a "did you know" blurb):

....
....
....
....

Issues (industry issues that customer can relate to and agree that they have experienced).

....
....
....
....

Gains (show positive gains of other people/companies from making a change).

....
....

....

....

Results (give an example of someone/ a client once you have permission from them to do so).

....

....

....

....

Propose to the reader that they can see similar positive results as well.

....

....

....

....

Contact (indicate that you will be contacting them soon so they'd know who you are when you call, even if they forget).

....

....

....

....

Generally, your e-mail or letters must flow in this order. It's like sending a long text message, people mostly first respond to the last thing you said or asked. It was the last thing that stood out to them. Here, you want them to know that you'd call them as a follow-up.

> *Note, the main purpose of the email or letter is not really to sell any of your products or services, but to really sell the idea that you're going to call them.*

> *We're selling a phone call/ conversation here.*

Have you seen the movie "The Wolf of Wall Street" with Leonardo DiCaprio? There's a part of the movie where he just started working in a penny stocks company and his first sales call blew the rest of the staff away when he closed a $4,000.00 sale worth of 40,000 shares. He was able to make reference to a letter that they received from the customer requesting information. This is an example of why I believe that sending content before making a call, is important. Your call would have a smoother flow. It's like you have a reason to call after all.

THE CALL

The call is important. It is your first point of direct contact with your prospective customer. Remember that insurance sales call script I mentioned earlier in this chapter? Remember how salesy it was? Remember how I was turned off by the word 'opportunity'?

I'm going to give you a structure that I developed over the years as a successful salesman. This was never planned or scripted. It was developed over time.

I did everything I was not supposed to when it came to calling people. I disrespected people's time. I disturbed and nagged them and was even shut down for calling someone at one time. In fact, I felt so horrible when I was told to never call back, that I stayed at home the next day from work. I felt ashamed although no one else in my office knew that's what I did! True story.

Over time I learnt a strategy by myself. I started thinking about what I should say exactly to people whenever I call. I tried this and I tried that. I monitored their responses over time and within three years I realised I developed somewhat of a script that was effective. But it worked best in tandem with an e-mail or letter I had sent previously.

You've got to be prepared because when you call, chances are that the intended recipient either got the correspondence, didn't look at it or never received it. You've got to be prepared to respond accordingly to that.

I recommend that through practice, this call would not last you more than 30 seconds. The less time I spend on the phone, the more effective I can be when I'm face to face.

NOTE: The objective of the email or letter was to sell a call, now the objective of the call, isn't to sell what you have, but to sell a meeting with the person.

Here's my script:

"Hi, is this Mr/Ms/Mrs _____?

Hi, my name is _____, I'm calling from _____. Did I catch you in a bad time?

I'm calling about the e-mail/letter I sent two days/two weeks ago about _____. Did you receive it?

Does this sound interesting to you?

Okay, let's meet to discuss this in more detail. Would next Wednesday at 10:00a.m., or, Thursday at 2:00p.m., be convenient for you?

Okay, would you mind if I send a calendar invite or text message as a reminder?

Have a great day."

What questions popped into your mind as you were reading? Well let me break down this 'first call script' for you and show you how it works every time. Now every conversation would flow differently. As long as you can come back to this script and keep the flow to the end to book a meeting, you have it made. But it's okay to go off-script. That's natural, that's normal. But you must work within certain parameters otherwise you'd lose control of the conversation and not get a meeting. As I said earlier, I did everything that didn't work. I guarantee that this is effective.

First line: "*Hi, is this Mr/Ms/Mrs* _____*?* Well, this is self-explanatory. You're making sure you have the correct person on the line. If not, I advise to request to speak to the person you'd want to in an assertive way. This is in case you meet "the gatekeeper" (or secretary who screens all calls).

If you were to politely ask to speak to your potential customer, or ask if they are in, or ask if they are available like saying something such as, "May I speak with Mr. Smith please?" you will most likely not get to them. The gatekeeper will question your motive and in most cases would not make the person available to you, and take a message or ask you to call back.

Instead do this, identify yourself and instruct the gatekeeper to transfer you. This develops an immediate impression in the mind of the gatekeeper or secretary that you and "the boss" knows each other well and possibly he or she is expecting your call. For instance, "Hi, this is Adrian from UPSELL, could you transfer me to Mr Smith?" Don't end the question in a high pitch or tone. That would sound like a question, even though it is. Your aim is to make it sound like an instruction. Keep it at a low tone. The immediate response would either be a question as to who is calling again or they would just say, "please hold".

Once the potential customer confirms it is he/she, or you are transferred from the secretary the next line is, *"Hi, my name is _____ and I'm calling from _____. Did I catch you in a bad time?"* You immediately identify who you are and where you are calling from which peaks interest in the mind of the receiver. Then you ask, "Did I catch you in a bad time?" to show respect for the potential customer's time. But there's a science that goes behind that question as well. I've been asked, "Adrian, why don't you say the words 'good time', isn't that negative to use the word 'bad'?" Actually, no. Think about this, if you're the receiver of the call and I ask you if I caught you in a 'good time', in most cases as a person, you already feel a sales pitch coming on and you begin to raise your 'bullshit screen' to ward off any 'bullshit' that could potentially be thrown at you. If I ask you "did I catch you in a bad time?" less likely you'd feel a sales pitch coming on and start to become either interested or concerned about what I have to say. This is how I know this line works when used that way.

In most cases the response to the question would be something to the effect of, "I have a couple minutes…" which indicates you can proceed to continue the call. If it really is not a good time, then apologise for the intrusion and ask what is a good time to return the call. Make sure and call back at that time given.

For the sake of this exercise, let's say you are able to proceed. The next line is *"I'm calling about the email/letter I sent two days/two weeks ago about _____. Did you receive it?"* You cut out any frilly stuff and salesy things and just get straight to the point in each sentence if you didn't notice by now. Now a couple things can happen here. Either:

- They got it.
- They got it and didn't get time to go through it.
- Or they didn't get it at all.

If they got it, you proceed to the next line *"Does this sound interesting to you?"* If they got it and didn't get time to go through it, or, they didn't get it at all, briefly state in about 15 words what it is about then proceed to the next line asking if it is interesting to them. Remember the aim is to be straight to the point.

Now, if it does not interest them, thank them for their time and end the call. You just disqualified a client who would have potentially wasted your time. Maybe they would be a good fit later down the road, but definitely not now. Spend more time with better prospects remember?

But if it does sound interesting, we proceed to the next line in the script *"Okay, let's meet to discuss this in more detail. Would next Wednesday at 10:00a.m., or Thursday at 2:00p.m., be available to you?"* The reason I immediately go straight into booking a meeting is really because I just got confirmation that my content interests them, and the best way to discuss it more, is in person, rather than over the phone. Also, I do not start discussing more about my products or service over the phone, because I could potentially be giving the client reasons why they should not meet with me. It would actually work to my disadvantage! We need to get our 'foot in the door' of their offices and when they say, 'it's interesting, you just got it. Don't step back by over-selling a reason to meet. Just step in by booking the meeting.

You will notice I then suggested two dates and times convenient to the customer's busy schedule and had shown respect for their time. Or did I?

What I actually did is make the customer feel that way. I gave him or her the impression I respected their schedule, but what I actually did was gave two specific times convenient with *my* schedule. I recommend you do this because you won't double book meetings or personal things with business things. Time management is key to successful selling in any area of business.

Here, two things are likely to happen

1. The client selects one of the times (remember to pause between the dates and times so the customer has enough time to process the thought). Wednesday at 10:00a.m., pause, or Thursday at 2:00p.m., or they say neither times are good.

2. If so, then ask what the available times on their schedule are. Only at this point you really give the customer control of something in the conversation. Then book one if convenient.

Finally, after all of this is done, we have to end the call with, "Okay, would you mind if I send a calendar invite or text message as a reminder?" At this point, because you already have a commitment to meet, they won't mind agreeing to a calendar invite, text message or e-mail (e-mails are not as effective because not everyone checks them in a timely manner when busy).

Just so you won't have to flip back to the script, here it is again:

"Hi, is this Mr/Ms/Mrs _____?

Hi, my name is _____ and I'm calling from _____. Did I catch you in a bad time?

I'm calling about the email/letter I sent two days/two weeks ago about _____. Did you receive it?

Does this sound interesting to you?

Okay, let's meet to discuss this in more detail. Would next Wednesday at 10:00a.m., or, Thursday at 2:00p.m., be available to you?

Okay, would you mind if I send a calendar invite or text message as a reminder?

Have a great day."

SUMMARY

- Prospecting is the lifeblood of any salesperson.
- When done diligently and accurately it is an essential ingredient for sales success.
- Quality time spent here will give you the best possible return on your investment.
- Always get contact information and make contact.
- Do not sell.
- Give free content.
- Introduce yourself as a problem solver.
- Do not give away all your information up front.
- Have adequate information about customer.
- Send some form of correspondence before calling anyone (e-mails or letters personally addressed unless you are into mass-mailing).
- Use the call script and in both correspondence and call, be straight to the point by cutting out most of the pleasantries and frills.
- Suggest two dates and times to book the meeting and always follow-up.

Go practice with someone. Go call real customers and see for yourself how it works. In fact, e-mail or send direct mail then call some new customers using the research techniques you received earlier in this chapter. You may fumble a bit in the beginning but eventually you'll get it smooth.

Start doing this, and once you have at least one meeting booked, only then you should begin reading the next chapter. I promise you, by the time you're at the end of this book, you'll be a master salesperson and negotiator.

CHAPTER 3

THE TRUST AND RELATIONSHIP

"The most important single ingredient
in the formula of success is knowing how
to get along with people."
~Theodore Roosevelt

Jim Rohn once said, "You cannot succeed by yourself. It's hard to find a rich hermit."

My good friend Tony J. Selimi sat down with me one day and shared this experience. From what he shares I can assure you that it has opened my eyes and taught me so much about dealing with people:

"Adrian, firstly I do not believe that we should build a relationship with an end in mind. In my opinion, the easiest way to build a trustworthy relationship is to 'show up' with another human being with your heart open. If that human being, in time, becomes part of something greater, that's fantastic, but if it doesn't, that's fantastic as well.

Let me share with you a great metaphor that explains the importance of trust and authenticity in relationship building and information sharing. If we want for two computers to have access to all of the data that is shared on a computer network, the first thing that needs to happen when they get connected is to be authenticated on that network. This is a necessary step for these two computers to be trusted in order for them to be able to access and share the information that is on that network. In a similar way, for two people to share information with one another their inner knowing needs to trust the other person.

First of all, each person must have an authentic relationship with themselves before they can be authentic with another person. If these two people are not honest with their own inner being, their sharing of information will be concealed with lies. If on the other hand they come to be with one another in an open, honest and authentic way, naturally they start to share information that normally they would not reveal.

The moral of the story is that people will share information if they trust you, you are authentic, and you have an inner awareness of your true being.

The problem arises because authenticity and our awareness constantly change as we go through the process of evolving our being. For instance, if we're going through something that we perceive as very difficult, for me this was in 2009 when I faced redundancy and was being forced out of a job that I loved, we will go through tremendous emotional upheaval.

If not dealt, these emotions can impact our well-being, our behaviours, and will prevent us from authentically sharing what is truly going on inside ourselves. Back then I decided to meet people who went through the same process to understand why so many were put through this process that destabilises their identity, creates fear, and leaves them feeling stressed.

Many of the people that I met back then, I realized much later down the line how they were meeting and communicating with me in the same negative vibration as the one I was in. It is the very same negative experience that gave birth to my desire to do something about the way I was feeling.

It is this innate desire, curiosity, and pain that forced me to go to one of Dr. John Demartini's talks and sign up to a few of his seminars, as deep down I was seeking a way out of my misery. If everyone around you speaks about their pain, it is certain that you will not get the solution hanging around people that feel disempowered, right?

If we want to find the solution to our personal, professional, and business problems, then it is up to us to change the environment and the people to the one that matches the pleasures we are seeking. In order to maximise our natural inbuilt intelligent wisdom we need to increase our own awareness to the vibration we want. If we want love then our inner vibration needs to match the one of love and above.

In this awareness that takes us out of our comfort zone and into experiences that can help us create opportunities, attend talks, and if you have a solution for the pain people experience create events for people to learn to grow through their life's greatest adversity. It is for this very same reason that I felt called to write my latest book "#Loneliness: The Virus of The Modern Age", to offer people a road map that leads them away from their struggles and into a path of success, health, wisdom and wealth.

One of those life changing events that put me on a new life trajectory was a talk by Dr. John Demartini's I decided to attend, when I felt broken. When I heard him speak it was as if he had gone into my head and was speaking to my thoughts, as if somebody had split me in half and the other half was John. Every word he was saying was matching my thoughts, they were words I loved speaking, and yet, I've never met this person before!

Being in John's presence I could easily compare how he was very different from the rest of the people in my daily environment where I was living. Having listened to his talk, I felt inspired from within.

My inner being knew that everything John was saying was from that place of inner truth, authenticity, and trust. I realised how his values are aligned to my true authentic values. From that place of authenticity, we ended up having a very nice conversation, it is this which inspired me to take action and book a consultation and attend his Breakthrough Experience.

I loved getting to know John; equally he got to know me, for what I stand for and what I am here to do in this life, we both shared from that authentic place within us. When I started my journey with Dr. John Demartini, I did it from honouring my highest values, from learning point of view. I did not go to his talk from 'what I'm going to get out of this guy' point of view.

I attended the talk because when I saw his video on YouTube, he was saying things in a way that my entire vibration felt it, and with every word spoken I felt I was soaked into a fountain of wisdom instantly. John was satisfying my urge for wisdom, whilst the pain that I used to have from working in various toxic environments in the corporate world pushed me into the direction of setting up my own business. I became an entrepreneur and started to show up in the world with a big mission to change, educate, and inspire the minds and elevate the hearts of one billion people. I developed the big vision that I had as a child, to deliver a solution for humanity to heal, love and connect in an authentic way. It is this innate knowing that helped me create **TJS Evolutionary Method : ALARM ®** *that I talk about in my Amazon best-selling book "A Path to Wisdom". A unique method that creates the body-mind-heart synchronisation was created to help people heal by following twenty five unique conscious engineering steps.*

Meeting John, was a great indication to my heart that I am on the right path. John was the mirror I was seeking, the one that showed me clearly that there is a man out there who was already doing his hearts work, I told myself, 'if he does it, so could I'.

This knowing really inspired me to go back for more and continue working with him to grow my coaching business. In doing so, in committing for many years to learn from this masterful teacher, I actually ended up building a really good rapport, a great relationship through being my true authentic self. It is by observing another person being extremely authentic that helps us raise our own awareness on the gifts we possess, in the way we communicate and show up in the world.

It is from that authenticity of showing up in each other's life with our hearts open and without any pre-set agenda that three years down the line, I approached Dr. Demartini and asked "would you write a foreword for my book?"

One of the busiest man on the planet instantly replied "Yes." Point being, three years prior to this, first of all I did not imagine that I would have written a book, secondly I would have not imagined I would get a praise from one of the top human behaviour experts of our times.

The truth is, I did not go to John's talk, seminars, and consultations with an agenda saying 'what I want from him or from this relationship.' I just went into every experience with him being my true authentic self, being there with my desire to grow and to help people and humanity. My heart, mind and soul was ready to bring something unique to the world that is aligned with my highest values which are learning, loving, growing, sharing and contributing.

It is when our values are truly aligned that we have true authentic transparent trustworthy relationships with others. It is from this space of inner alignment that information becomes easily exchanged between two parties, and where both sides are creating a 'win-win' position in every exchange that happens between them.

If we want to relate the above to sales training, when the values of the sales person, company and customer are aligned and all parties are taught how to communicate authentically with one another, they don't have to sell anything. The information itself, the intelligence of the information being exchanged, and the trust built among the various parties will do the selling.

From this trustworthy relationship that we had built over time that John wrote the foreword for what became award-winning and international best-selling book A Path to Wisdom and later on my next book #Loneliness. Both books helped me create a global credibility and trust with my audience.

Being my true self is what led to having one of the world's number one experts in Human Behaviour endorsing my work, have a great relationship with Dr. John Demartini, and openly promote his work to all of my clients.

Coming from a place of service created a very beautiful mutual partnership which, back when I met him, I could have never thought I would really be able to relate to a man who is a billionaire! In my mind I would think "who am I for a billionaire to want to connect with me?" You know, back then I felt extremely small in comparison to a billionaire, but now, many years down the line I don't!

You know, a lot of people go into relationships with agendas, but in my opinion the most beautiful relationship that we can create is the one that evolves over time and the one with ourselves. With that way of thinking, being and living you can go to seminars and form unique bonds with random strangers.

You can read many books about sales, building authentic relationships, or how to create what most people want-financial freedom. The truth is, this way of learning would only unlock about 10% of your worth, I believe when you work with a great coach who can be a clean mirror you can unlock the other 90% of your worth.

Reason being, seminars, talks, videos and books are one-way learning system with no bidirectional feedback. But if you work with someone who is a great teacher in your life, they can help you unlock the other 90% so that you can accelerate your growth and maximise your human potential.

I believe if every human being had an excellent teacher, our world would be a much better world, we would move towards a more conscious way of leading, living, and loving one another. To be the best, I believe it is a necessity to invest in the best teachers that elevate you to a whole new level of awareness.

Like it or not, people who say that they don't have money for personal development are the very same people who spend their money on cars, holidays, clothes, food, cigarettes, alcohol, expensive birthdays, marriage ceremonies, and many other different things that they value.

In contrast, people who value learning, growth, as well as their big vision they invest in their personal and professional development. Remember this piece of valuable advice that I teach all of my clients to help them save time, people who don't value what you have to offer, they'll give you excuses, either change your offer and find people who want it, or know their worth and therefore adjust your offer to match that. Make sure you know your worth, in doing so you radiate value in everything that you say and do.

When people want to sell something, if the person who sells does not know how to communicate in the language that supports the highest values of the other person, they will not be able to close a sale!

But if the sales person through listening can immediately pick up the values of the person he is trying to sell too, then their values are aligned and the sale happened naturally. You do not sound like you're selling something, instead you are perceived as someone who is caring for their needs and see you as someone who understands their problem and has a genuine solution for their problem, that's the true art of heart selling and sales winning.

If I were to simplify my relationship with Demartini, I'd say I have an extremely loving relationship with him. He run's his business, I run my business, but I also have that heart-loving relationship with him where exchange of value happens. You may be wondering, how do I benefit from this relationship, he is not buying my products, I am.

Well, this is the tricky part to bring to our awareness the unseen value in every relationship you forge. In my case I benefit from John in millions of ways! Anybody who knows Demartini, will know of me too. Then you may ask how does then John benefit from me? Well, every reader who he is not potentially reaching that I'm reaching will also know of him.

Meaning, everybody who knows about my book, they will instantly know about all of my teachers, clients and people who helped me become what I am known today as a speaker, coach, and a world renowned human behaviour expert.

I love to openly talk about who my teachers, coaches and healers have been. I love sharing the work of all the therapists and all the people who have actually helped me transform my life and helped me become a global entrepreneur, leader, and an expert in my field. It is with gratitude that I share them all as they for sure became my mirror to unlock the true value I had in me.

Nowadays, I do not have much time to go to seminars as I run my own talks, seminars and workshops. I remain focused to deliver my vision and mission. This is the shift that happened in me from working one to one with my teachers. I see many people who go to seminars and who continue to go to seminars but they are not creating the results they deep down are seeking. Many people end up living uninspired lives without ever truly living their true potential.

What matters in every relationship you build especially the one where the person you are meeting is highly respected expert is to leave with a knowing that whatever was shared between you two was of massive value, a value you normally may have had to pay top notch to receive. The more authentic you become, the more you know that your life already transformed the moment you met that person and entered that relationship.

So for me, relationship building is really about our inner journey, it is about our authentic being, showing up in our greatness with every human being that we meet. This way of living requires for you to have done your inner work and acknowledged to yourself that you already are in your greatness. Otherwise, the relationship you build with people would be based according to the façades, according to the awareness you have in that present moment.

The more you are in the awareness of being in the present moment, the less pain you will experience in that relationship. If you are in a poverty mind-set, you will meet people who are also in that poverty mind-set. The reason people hang around people with low self-worth to be *validated that they don't need to challenge themselves, to make that change, to step into their greatness.*

They do this in order to feel good about themselves, because this other person is not challenging them. But if you meet a person who is extremely wealthy, and you are in the poverty mind-set, they would challenge all your buttons!

Reason being is because you know you are not living in your greatness, your inner being that is infinite knows this too! A lot of people tell me they are 'living in their greatness', yet they have financial problems, they hide away from sharing their account balance, they're overweight, feel stressed, and to most questions asked that challenges their comfort zone there's no answer coming back.

A lot of people I come across in my day to day living tell me that they are the best spiritual teacher that is out there, and when asked how wealthy are they respond with "Ah, spirit is not about wealth", "wealth is not important, spirit is,"etc. For me spirit without matter is expressionless, matter without spirit is motionless. Thus, people who bridge the spirit with matter are those teachers who are spiritually and materially wealthy, they tend to manifest anything they think of and live healthy and happy.

There are many people out there who want something, but there are very few who know what they want, are authentic, and know how to get it. Recently, I met a lady at an event I was speaking, and before she even came close I could feel her aggression, anger, and discomfort radiating out of her as she was walking towards me.

What happened was, on that night, a client of mine who I have helped through her journey of healing her breast cancer publicly shared with everybody how I helped her develop a healing mind-set. She even mentions me in her book No Sugar, My Journey My Choice and how through every coaching and healing session by using my TJS Evolutionary Method I helped her shift her limiting beliefs, create a healing mind-set, and aligned her values with her day to day life. How this work in combination with her medical treatment helped her get back to perfect health.

When she spoke to me her attitude was one of attack, judgments, and without ever knowing about my work accusing me how can I help someone who is diagnosed with cancer if I am not a medic. She went on to say, how can I help a cancer patient better then she can. She angrily said, "Well you're not a doctor, how can you advise a patient?"

I smiled and responded with certainty, "If you are willing to pay for the time required to give you in depth explanation of my work I would happily sit down with you for few days and explain how the conscious engineering processes of the TJS Evolutionary Method have healed hundreds of people who sought my help for all sort of issues." She got even more angry as I went to say, "It surprises me to see a wonderful soul such to behave in an accusative way towards another professional. It's a shame that your pain and arrogance precedes your beautiful intelligence I see in your eyes."

She instantly stopped talking and started to listen. I went on to say "if these words ring true to you, get back to me, book a consultation and let's have a discussion on why you are so angry.". She shook hands with me, asked for my card and she left without saying anything else. Few days down the line we had a consultation. Moral of this story, if people approach people with arrogance, you're not going to create authentic relationship if you are not authentic with them and if you are not going to communicate with your highest expression of yourself. She knew I spoke the truth, it is this truth that her inner knowing picked up, and it me standing up to her that created a trustworthy relationship that lead for her later on to became a client of mine.

Most sales people I have trained, the first thing I did is to help them see how **not** to enter into a relationship by being arrogant, by telling to themselves, "I'm a salesman, I know how to sell." Instead, I taught them tools to be better listeners, to not assume that they know something about the other person listening at the other side of the line, and to be able to go into a meeting with certainty about the value they bring as the expert in their chosen field.

To be a great sales person, don't assume anything about the person you are trying to sell to, go into a conversation with *them and become an active listener. Usually through listening to everything people will tell you learn everything you need to know about them and what it is that they need of you.*

Building trustworthy relationship is extremely important part to every sale and yet most people do it wrongly as they do not show up in the conversation in an authentic way. They tend to show off different masks they have built over the many years. The truth is, we all have different masks, but some masks are extremely dirty, tight, and do not fit us very well.

People who have done a lot of inner work, they start the process of peeling off those masks, in doing so they begin to reveal more of their true authentic self. The more they do this, the more love radiates out of them, and the more people they meet become active listeners.

For instance Brendon Burchard, he talks about how to influence people through building a strong mind-set. I talk about how to influence people through the power of being present. This is the journey I take my clients who are high achievers, influencers and celebrities so that they become a magnetic force of light that draws people in.

To be this force of light requires for you to overcome many issues buried deep within your subconscious self. This inner journey is not a one of process, it is a constant evolution process, and hence why I believe in continued education, development, and learning. Despite the fact that I am considered by many people an expert in my field, some say I am a wise soul, and others pay me a lot of money to work with me privately, I am constantly investing in my development and I'm surrounded by my two teachers, mentors and healers. I love learning, constantly evolving, and learning new skills that I can apply every day to grow myself and my clients' businesses and to make sure I constantly add more value in people's lives.

Relationship is a word used by many people, what you may want to become aware about is from what levels of awareness you are using this word, is it from one where you are imposing yourself to forcefully build a relationship or from one that is authentic, genuine, and is heart driven.

By design we are intelligent beyond our imagination, beyond what our mind can perceive, and our emotions can detect. The very same intelligence that build us already knows the true building blocks of an authentic relationship that is trustworthy in which information is shared freely and service is exchanged. It is this intelligence that already knows if what you are communicating is authentic, or not before you even first open your mouth.

Unfortunately, most people do not know thyself, therefore they cannot build authentic relationship with others. A great metaphor that I use for this is mobile phones. The moment we switch them on they already have a relationship with the entire world. Although we do not see any wires connected to it, we are connected wirelessly to an information *super highway in which we have access to trillions of bits of information that are being shared daily.*

We operate exactly in the same way, our aura, energy field communicates with others wirelessly and we are subjected to all the information that is shared by every human being. We are living in a web of collective consciousness where if we tune our inner being to the right frequency we can access the information that resides in this super conscious highway freely and create our desired outcomes. In the thin air that we are surrounded daily lives an unseen world of information, by heightening and calibrating our senses we can tap into the wisdom that lives hidden away from our limited awareness."

Award winning Author, Speaker, and Human Behaviour expert internationally known as The See-Through Coach.

Tony J. Selimi is internationally known as a Human Behaviour, Cognition and Emotional Intelligence Expert. To his clients he is known as the 'See-Through' coach and specialises in assisting people find solutions to their personal, professional and business problems, accelerate their learning, and achieve excellence in all of the eight key areas of life:

spiritual, mental, emotional, physical, business, money, relationship and love-heart intelligence.

More about the author: http://tonyselimi.com

As a business consultant he globally provides answers to questions and practical solutions to life's challenges in talks, workshops, one to one coaching, mastermind groups, retreats, articles, radio and TV interviews as well as through his books and online downloads of the TJS Evolutionary Meditation Solutions.

His clients are entrepreneurs, leaders, and people from all walks of life who seek his help to manifest their highest vision, to be more healthy, wealthy, wise, spiritual and influential. They range from Celebrities, MPs, Dr's, Scientists, Coaches, to CEO's and Managers of FTSE 100 companies such as Micros Tony is no stranger to the media, appearing in various national magazines including *Soul and Spirit, Global Women, Science to Sage, Migrant Women, Accelerate Your Business, Changing Careers Magazine, Consciousness Magazine, Your Wellness, Time Out, Soul Mate Relationship World Summit;* TV and radio shows including ABC, NBC, CBS, Fox,

Hay House, Voice of America, Radio Macedonia, Untangled FM, Self-Discovery Radio and Spirit Radio.

He gives inspirational talks on a range of topics including, importance of women in leadership, value-driven leadership, entrepreneurship, the evolution of consciousness, peace, well-being, alternative methods of healing, the impact loneliness has on global health, how to be paid your worth, activating heart's intelligence and on various issues we face globally.

Tony has been a keynote speaker at the Animas Coaching Institute, the Yes Group, Blue Cow Summit, Raw Fest, Be Inspired, Conscious Leadership Events, private functions, and Mind Body Spirit festivals. He hosts regular webinars with his clients entitled 'Conversations with Your Highest Expression of Your Self' for, SAP, Bank of America, E&Y, Vandercom and Deutsche Bank.

Tony is known for creating amazing transformation and leaving his clients feeling inspired, empowered, peaceful, and reconnected to the infinite wisdom of love.

What can I possibly say that could top what Tony just shared with us? I believe that he was even authentic in sharing his experiences with us so much that I felt inspired while I was typing it here for you to read. Later on in this chapter, I would begin sharing some really amazing techniques that would not only help you from within, but externally, you'd be using the body language that matches the professional that you are. The body language that would add to the amazing first impression you are going to set with that new client you will meet.

Let me share another experience with you. I want to tell you about Nienke Van Bezooijen. Nienke is an Inspirational Keynote Speaker, International Master-Trainer and Author. Nienke is also an established international TEDx Speaker coach in the Netherlands and works in English and Dutch. To expand the reach of helping speakers worldwide she developed her own training.

But before Nienke reached this point, there were things she needed to do. Here is her amazing story as told by her:

"I've had challenges all my life. I've been very ill, I've been paralysed at one point, became a single mom after two very difficult pregnancies. I was, as we call it in the Netherlands a 'job hopper' where I hopped every two years to another job to make it fit with my personal life. It wasn't easy. But, my mom always says that as soon as I started to talk, I would

say "I would do it myself, don't worry". Those were my first words after 'mummy' and 'daddy'. I always liked going for whatever I wanted to do.

After twenty five years working in healthcare and as a healthcare manager, I did my MBA in the evening hours. When I had my MBA, I thought I knew everything about Business, so much so that I had a big fight with my boss because I was educated more than he was. That wasn't a good thing for him. So there and then I decided that I will do it myself! I don't need bossy managers, I would become an entrepreneur. I have my MBA, and I will start my consultancy business. I was so blank, so naive, I thought I knew everything about business but, that's not running your own business. That's analysing someone else's business. Nothing, nothing, nothing to do with entrepreneurship.

In 2008, hand by hand I found out in the financial crisis that my MBA wasn't the same thing as entrepreneurship. I started to take entrepreneurial courses. What do I do as an entrepreneur? The first place I started working in was in helping others manage themselves at work, basically in the HR field. I was quite good at it but not happy.

After a while I was asked to help set up businesses so I made a company about 'Business Resultancy'. That didn't quite work out well because I was known as a healthcare manager. I found out the hard way that just jumping out and saying I was a 'consultant' doesn't work. Because people want to see you and your results, and then they buy from you. And if you just have a nice logo, it doesn't work. You have to show results and walk the talk!

Looking back, I realised why it didn't work when I connected all the dots. I still was not doing what was the right fit. One of my largest clients who hired me as a business consultant asked me to develop training and deliver it around the topic of Autism. A quite specific field. They wanted to train people who wanted to become an autism coach. I dove right in, developed a training, made it in to a certificate training and started to train and educate people and I realised that I loved it! I loved it far more than the whole consultancy work. I started looking for other types of training and joined a 'Train the Trainer' programme in London. I was invited to join the master class making the stage in Thailand and working directly with T. Harv Eker and Blair Singer. They are very salesy guys. As a former nurse, it was a very tough thing to do because it didn't resonate with me.

I like to inspire people, to enrol people into how they can benefit. That is what led to sales. Far better than what I call the 'Tell-Sell' method. From there, I started working with a voice coach and she inspired me to work with people and help them to speak well in the speaking field. I did her program 'Find Your Million-Dollar Voice', and she's a woman, which was a difference for me. Because as a woman I know that we sell in a different way than the 'masculine way'. It's softer, it's more friendly, it's more, "oh,if you're friends with me we can do business" like 'girl-talk'. It's a whole different world compared to tough selling.

The only person I know who is good at it is a woman from the United States called Lisa Sessofitch, because she does really well in sales in a 'feminine' way. I started my third company 'Presentation Master', and now I'm doing what I really love. I even joined the Professional Speakers Academy with Andy Harrington (who endorsed this book as well). That's where I also learned how to reach my goals by having great content that can lead to sales. I love to give value. Value first is what I would encourage anyone who would want to succeed in sales or any area of their lives. Because I don't believe in pushing your opinion on someone else. I believe in enrolment. If I can enrol you into another world or vision the sales will come from there.

Rapport is key in the whole thing, and if I talk from the heart, it's not about ME, but what I can do for you (the customer). It's about listening, enrolling, that's the important part. Since I have been working that way, I have stopped all marketing, everything. I believe in the personal touch and what I can do for you in the relationship. Trust me, it's worth it. You get the best referrals and endorsements, and I work with the best clients who pays really well.

The real connection and relationship will outperform what any kind of marketing can do.

Nienke and I are good friends and have been in contact with each other for some time.

As professionals who help others both individually and in their companies, we also support each other's work and achievements.

I recommend you visit her website www.presentationmaster.com and get a copy of her book *The Speaker Success Solution* if you are interested in a speaking career.

What have you gathered from Nienke's experiences? This is where we are going to start this chapter. We are going to understand not just what we need to do in order to build rapport and trust, but also how we are going to do it and most importantly, why? Nienke became genuinely interested in other people who helped her grow her business significantly. I recommend that if you become interested in people, you'd see success much sooner than if you were to only focus on money.

Let's go a little deeper. Why do we need relationships? How does this benefit us? How does this benefit helps others? Think about that for a moment, seriously.

The basis of customer loyalty and repeat business, lies in building long-term relationships. That's how it benefits us. What we also do is we help make it easier for our customers to make decisions in achieving their goals as well. It's definitely a two-way street.

Now the basis of building a relationship starts with the simple things. Many times I have noticed that people forget these simple things and focus on only a few which makes relationship-building with others feel like a task. If you always remember to genuinely do these simple things, it would also be easy for you to work with others. We must always remember to smile, be kind, feel love for others, show genuine concern to help others, being friendly, showing respect, shaking hands, being open-minded and no matter what happens, remembering that things always work out in the end.

When you actively try building relationships with others, you build rapport quickly, gain the other person's trust as well as their confidence in you. This is also a powerful tool that good salespeople apply because they are able to close more sales with much less effort.

To begin building trust and a relationship with another person, we need to remember that in business we need to do it fast! In order to do this, you need to be able to communicate your ability to bring value to the other person at each step of the process.

I remember very well there was a movie called "Tommy Boy" with David Spade and Chris Farley. There was this one scene where they were brake pad salesmen and went to a client's office and before they were able to build any kind of rapport or relationship, Chris tried telling a story using the client's collection of cars as props (which were important to the client) and destroyed them in the process. Not a good thing to do because they were thrown out of the office!

There's no question that people do business with people they like, and the key to having someone like you, is to first build rapport with them!

At this point, I'm going to start giving you techniques that you would be able to actively use when you meet a client face-to-face. You already have a call script that works, now let's take it to another step.

Note* some ground rules. Here are four things that you need to do in order to effectively become an expert in your field when selling or doing business:

- *Try to talk about things that other people are interested in. People love to talk about themselves and what they like. Do some research.*

- *Get into a rhythm with them as well. Appreciate the things they like.*
- *Empathy. Use it. Be understanding.*
- *Find commonality in the process. Things that you both have in common. Not obvious things like a brand of shoes or handbag but hobbies or so.*

THE GREETING

Depending on the type of business you have, whenever you meet a new client, the greeting is relatively the same, however, the approach may be different in the situations. I can split that up into two areas for you. Either, you have a retail outlet that depends on walk-in customers, or your business or place you work, requires you to actively pursue new customers. In-house sales or field-sales.

Let's work with the simpler one first. In-house sales in a Retail Business. Here we depend on mostly walk-in customers. How do you usually experience a greeting if you were to walk into a clothing store for instance? In most cases I have experienced this type of greeting:

"Hi, need some help?" or *"Hi, are you getting through?"*

What is the most popular response to that?

It goes mostly like:

"No, thanks." or *"Just looking."* or *"It's okay, I'm getting through."*

What happened there is the sales person or sales clerk asked a closed ended question that required either a 'yes' or 'no' response. I believe that because the sales person is either lazy or intimidated to work with other people that they are afraid the person actually needs assistance, in so doing asks a question that would give them the hope the customer would say no, or they also give off a vibe or aura that they really do not want to help. Either way, they still want a sale, they still want commissions. If you are not willing to actively work, how can you expect to be paid?

As a customer, when you ask me that type of question as a greeting, I do not want to be disturbed. I want to walk around your store by myself. I do not want to feel like you're going to follow me around. I want to feel comfortable knowing that you are not going to try to sell me something!

That's it! The way in which the approach is done, the way in which the greeting is said, already feels salesy! I would not want to deal with a salesperson if I feel as though I would be sold something, because I do not want to be bothered, and if you 'force' me to buy something, I do not want to experience buyer's remorse of having something I do not need or something that is faulty!

How can we as salespeople have an approach that does the opposite? How can we have a greeting that comes across as genuine, as helpful, in a non-threatening, non-salesy way?

I've discovered that people feel more comfortable when asked an open-ended type of question that requires a response other than 'yes' or 'no'. What I mean by open-ended? I mean, a question that requires an explanation as a response.

Here's how I train people in organisations on how to greet in a retail environment:

> *"Hi! Welcome to UPSELL Business Solutions. My name is Adrian. How may I help you?"*

If that's too long for you, leave out the part with your name. Imagine that for a second. If you walked into any establishment and you received a greeting like that, what would be your chances of telling that person a 'no'? Chances are, you'd say what you're there for won't you? (Providing you're not shopping or looking around). If you already know what you want, you'd probably say it anyways.

This opens the forum for dialogue! A conversation. Communication. This is the science behind the communication techniques I train people on. It's the same retail environment, but two different responses from two different types or greetings.

If you offer services and not just products off a shelf, a handshake would also be most appropriate. Which brings me to my next point; *the handshake.*

Did you know that there's a perfect professional handshake? What would you think about if I were to ask you 'what's the best way to give a handshake?'

In most cases when I ask that question, I get responses like:

- It must be firm.
- Eye contact.
- Same grip as the other person.
- Must not squeeze their hand.
- Your hand should be straight (palm facing one side).

Those are good answers, and some of them are very useful. I am not discounting those points. I agree with them. The last point I would question, however.

In my experience in communication and psychology studies, I discovered that the handshake reveals in an instant, the type of person you are. It's the first part of the first impression you'll set with anyone. And we all know there's no second chance to making a good first impression (although people's minds and feelings can change).

Have you ever shaken someone's hand but when they were extending their hand towards yours, their palm was facing downwards and coming from above their waist height, down into your hand? Picture that for a second. Did you see it happening? Did they feel 'big' to you?

That was a power play. It's not a conscious decision by the way. It's just natural for them and they don't realise it. It states power. 'I'm Bigger than you, more important, richer, smarter, faster, more powerful'.

The direction your palms face gives off the impression of the type of person you are. Now the power play can also display confidence. Which is really good. But not good if you want to make a first impression, especially, if you want to do business.

What you want to do is to give the other person the 'power play' move. In other words, when you extend your hand for a handshake, you need to have your palm facing slightly upwards (diagonally) so that when they are about to receive your handshake, they position their palm in a power play angle for a second.

They would feel good. But what it also does for you is give off the impression of openness. When you approach someone with open arms, you are embracing them. Even with an open palm handshake. It would say that you are open. Open minded, you have an open heart and they can talk to you about anything.

Approaching the other person with a handshake that's open also gives you the ability to read the type of personality of the other person. You'd know if you actively gave them the power play move, or if they naturally do that. You also get to see if they are open as well in the event that they do approach with an open palm.

No need to worry if both of you approach each other with open palms, when you make contact, it would be a natural normal handshake. But the impression would be made.

What confirms the handshake as the perfect handshake is also a smile, with eye contact and saying hello or exchanging names while the hands are clasped together for the shake. Don't look at your hand or anywhere else. I recommend you find someone right now and practice this.

The second type of greeting is different. We already dealt with the retail store type of greeting, but what about if you're 'on the field' and have to go out and meet new customers?

Let's say, you used the correspondence letter/e-mail, made the appointment using the telephone call script, and now you have to go to the meeting at the client's office.

You're there waiting to enter the client's office. What's on your mind?

Don't worry. I understand what it feels like to have some level of nervousness before entering any meeting. I still get that to this day at times. But I remind myself that I am always in control using this technique. And it works.

Remember, the appointment is already made, so when you enter, it's not always necessary to introduce your name again. Let's take control of this.

Approach the client after entering his/her office with your arm extended just before you are in front of them, for the handshake (palm facing slightly upwards at an angle). Make sure you're smiling and have good eye contact that's not in a weird way. Be genuinely happy to meet them. Exchange pleasantries and do not sit until you are asked to have a seat. So far, so good?

It is at this point we will begin using the face-to-face techniques. Now remember, this book give you the techniques in any sales training program you will experience. It's the style of teaching that would be different. But all sales are the same and most sales programs teaches the same sales process. What you're reading is my style, a little more in depth into 'why' and 'how' it works as well.

As soon as you are seated or while you are about to place your butt on the seat, you need to do something that would start building the rapport immediately and quickly. If you do not do this, you would lose the customer from the start, but if you do this and do it right, it would be a huge success to helping you engage your customer.

STARTING THE MEETING

First things first, you must always be in control of the conversation. If you are not in control of the conversation, then the customer is. You need to manage the control by staying within certain parameters, but if you let go, you would lose the control. How do you keep a conversation controlled while trying to achieve your goals? By asking questions, which helps control the conversation and the direction it goes. Once you know how to use this effectively, you are skilled. But it comes with a package. In order to do this right, you also need to be a good listener. Listen for needs. Listen for hints of what the customer may need so you can provide a healthy and beneficial

Sent E-mail/Letter

Phone Call

- Introduce
- If it's a bad time
- Reference to e-mail/letter
- Interesting?
- Set meeting with two date options

Start meeting

- Greeting
- Grab Attention

solution and do business.

Let me share a brief breakdown of what you have done so far. We will build onto this as you continue to read this book and you can use these as your guides or points to remember the flow of the process.

Let's begin the meeting. Just as you're about to sit or already seated, you need to grab the attention of the customer so as to get their minds off from what they are doing and onto you. This is very important because you do not want your customer to be thinking about other things while you are trying to have a conversation with them. It would complicate things from the very start and make it a lot harder and take a lot longer for you to close the sale.

You need to engage the customer and get them focused. You need to put the customer into a state of awareness and get them thinking strategically.

How do we grab their attention? Well there are four ways you can grab a customer's attention. You just need one. The most appropriate one based on the situation or what you've researched about the customer.

COMPLIMENT THE CUSTOMER

Give them a compliment they would not hear from someone else. You instantly grab their focus because you begin speaking about them and, it's something that's going to make them feel good.

For example, "I would like to commend you on your successful health fair you and your company executed last month. It was well received by the public and I believe the impact it had really did help many as well as looked really good for your corporate social responsibility initiative."

ASK THE CUSTOMER A CATCHY QUESTION

Ask a unique question that requires some thought to answer. When you get someone thinking hard about a situation or something interesting, you achieved the art of engagement from the start.

For example, "What would you do if your machinery was stolen? How would you track it?"

MENTION A REFERRAL

Using the name of someone who the customer knows well and has a good rapport with, can work to your advantage. Make sure that the customer has a good rapport with the referral's name you intend on using first, otherwise it would work to your disadvantage.

For example, "Your good friend Mark complimented our services and suggested that I contact you to see if you would be interested."

SAY SOMETHING AMAZING

A 'did you know' or a piece of information that is engaging or something the general public may not know that can capture someone's attention. You want an intrigued reaction from them where you know you've got their attention. For example, "Did you know that some of our cars here at BMW do not carry a spare tyre?"

What happens in addition to grabbing attention is that it prevents you from starting a talk about yourself or your company. Immediately, if you came into my office and started talking like that I'd think. "Oh gosh, this guy/girl wants to sell me something and I ain't buying."

Customers are interested in themselves. People on a whole are interested in themselves! They want to know 'what's in it for them?' Why would you begin any conversation in relation to yourself or what you do?

Sometimes, this may happen. A customer may say, "Tell me more about your company/what you do."

Talk briefly, give your elevator pitch line of who you are and immediately end the statement with a question. Try shifting focus away from speaking about yourself. It can be detrimental to sale in the end because you would give the customer enough time to formulate his or her idea of you before you make a good impression. Focus on them.

What you have just started by using one of these attention grabbers is a conversation unrelated to the purpose of the meeting. You are here building rapport on some form of common ground. The conversation here can go on for a short time or a long time. Eventually, you'd have to get down to the nitty gritty of the meeting.

Before you get into the real 'meat' of the meeting I want you to remember that you need to speak in accordance to how a customer would think if they were to buy something. Remember you too, are a customer yourself, and speaking about your benefits, features and advantages does not always sell. Here's an exercise I guarantee that would help you discover and remember how a customer thinks, and you can speak directly to them in that language.

The below illustrates a benefit or feature of what you sell (underlined). On the right, shows what the customer actually buys in relation to that point. I have placed some examples for you on random information, but once you see the flow I recommend you continue the list, but with your services or product features and benefits. When you have to speak to someone, use the language on the right and not necessarily your features and benefits that are on the left because people are interested in what's in it for themselves.

'Product/Service's Feature or Benefit' vs 'What the customer actually buys'

Run Flat Tires on a BMW – The safety and peace of mind knowing I don't have to stop to change a flat in a dangerous area/ bad weather.

Lemon scented (Home cleaning product) – The fresh scent that is easy on the nostrils as well as the ability to 'feel' clean in the surroundings.

Two Years Warranty – The service and peace of mind knowing that I would be covered or protected in the event of a manufacturer's defect with the product, and I would not be left unattended at my own cost at that time.

Highly Trained Staff – The peace of mind of, having competent, knowledgeable people who are professional and would know how to help in the event of any situation.

Please write a few of yours now

Great! Now you should have a better understanding of what people actually buy and how to speak with them using the right words.

Now I'd like you to recap what we've done so far in communicating with the customer. Please find a colleague and practice this. We will continue to add-on more content and strategy as you read on in this book.

Sent E-mail/Letter

Phone Call

- Introduce
- If it's a bad time
- Reference to e-mail/letter
- Interesting?
- Set meeting with two date options

Start meeting

- Greeting
- Grab Attention

Remember the telephone script. Try to stay on course with it. Now, not all conversations may be the same as the script. If you do have to go off-course, try to come back to the script.

ESTABLISHING THE OBJECTIVE OF THE MEETING

It is at this point, after you have successfully grabbed the attention of the customer, and created a conversation unrelated to the purpose of the meeting that you now get down to the purpose of the meeting!

When you establish the objective, a couple things happen; you are prepared both mentally and in the eyes of the customer, you come across as very organised and you also come across as very interested in the customer. People do business with you when you show interest in them. Grabbing their attention opens that tone for your meeting.

Establishing the objective of the meeting involves just three things. Is it easy to remember to do just three things? I hope so. These three things gives you the ability to lead the conversation and take control. You would lead the sales process. It can be written, memorised or you can even come up with it in the moment! Yes, on the spot.

It is a statement that includes:

- Your customer's benefit directly related to the said meeting you're in.
- An agenda of things to discuss in bullet point form.
- A notion, question or suggestion to move to the first point on the agenda.

Once you establish the objective especially in this sequence, it positions you as the authority, you are able to lead the conversation in any direction you'd like. You will be more believable and customers would be more open to listen when it is your time to speak.

E.g., *"We're here today to discuss <u>lowering staff turnover at your sub office,</u>"*

Which includes:
<u>*Your present issues*</u>   *Benefit*
<u>*Your H.R. policies*</u>
<u>*Who are the persons responsible at this time*</u> ◄——— *Agenda*
and <u>What do you intend to achieve in making any changes</u>.

Is there anything you'd like to ◄——————— *continue*
<u>add before we continue</u>?"

If you observe carefully the example I wrote above, you'd see the three parts of establishing the objective. It is short, simple and easy to follow. It will also be said in about 12 seconds. If you add too much more words to it or use too many filler words, you would not come across as prepared as well as you'd open your customer's mind to question you too early in the process.

It begins at this point where you need to start listening to what your customers really want instead of trying to figure out what they want. At this point you need to be genuinely interested in the customer, listen, really listen that is, and when you speak, speak from their perspective, ask questions to better your understanding of their situation (we will go into this more in the next chapter) and always focus on what the customer is saying to understand their needs.

Sent e-mail/letter

Phone Call

- Introduce
- If it's a Bad time
- Reference to e-mail/letter
- Interesting?
- Set meeting – 2 date options

Start meeting

- Greeting
- Grab attention

Small Talk

Establish the Objective

- Customer's benefit

Just as you practiced earlier with someone, or by yourself. Use the column on the left and add on the 'establishing objective of the meeting' part. Basically, after the small talk from grabbing their attention, you get right down to discussing business.

SUMMARY

- You cannot succeed by yourself. It's hard to find a rich hermit.
- Be authentic in your approach when meeting people. They 'pick up' on your aura.
- The basis of customer loyalty and repeat business, lies in building long-term relationships.
- You need to be able to communicate your ability to bring value to the other person at each step of the process.
- Try to talk about things that other people are interested in.
- Get into a rhythm with them as well.
- Empathy. Use it. Be understanding.
- Find commonality in the process.
- Use the proper welcoming if you have a retail store.
- Remember the handshake (palm slightly upwards).
- If going into a meeting, do the proper greeting.
- Grab the customer's attention to create rapport using 'small talk'.
- Establish the objective using the benefit, agenda and ask if it's okay to continue.

Go practice with someone. Go interact with real customers and see for yourself how it works.

CHAPTER 4

DEVELOPING
THE PASSION

*"Make your goals so big and inspiring,
that they make your problems seem
insignificant by comparison."*

~Andy Harrington

By the end of this chapter, you will learn certain techniques that would help you develop a passion in the hearts and minds of your clients.

Passion. How would you define passion? Are you passionate about something? Someone? Somewhere? Somehow? Let me share an interesting story about passion and how you can apply it in your work and what you do.

Andy Harrington is a good friend of mine. I have known him for a couple of years and I consider his teachings very useful. So useful that it makes him my mentor in the work that I do. Since I facilitate training sessions, I need to have certain skills in, not just presenting, but speaking and basically selling to an audience. The process is very different when you have to work with groups rather than a one-to-one basis.

However, Andy's experiences has given him the ability to develop a passion in people. Build or light that spark in people's hearts to take action.

Here's Andy's story on having a passion and how his passion is transferred to others. You can do this too if you just follow the steps throughout this book. As said by him, this is what he told me for the purpose of this chapter:

"Adrian, in 2009 I was sleeping on the floor of my mum's one bedroom retirement home following a failed business venture. To cap it all, my wife of 10 years then left me choosing to sleep with someone else.

I was always a good speaker and dreamed of being on a big stage. I heard about an event taking place at the London O2 Arena to 8000 people but was told there was no way I would get on the speaking bill as I didn't know the promoter and I also wasn't a big time speaker. I formed a plan.

I befriended one of the speakers that was speaking. I went out of my way to help him to improve his speaking skills. I suggested he help me get on the speaking bill for a small commission on sales and he agreed. We formed a plan.

I sent a DVD of my speaking at a small event of 150 people, showing my ability to speak and sell. I met with the promoter I wanted to get in touch with, with my speaker friend. Just like that, through determined efforts, I got the speaking opportunity at the London o2 Arena.

On the day, my talk was for one hour at 8:30a.m. Unfortunately, the audience thought the start time was 9:00a.m. At 8:30a.m., I walked out to empty chairs. Imagine how that felt. Like I had a big sinking feeling on the inside. However, after a few minutes, people started to come in, little by little the room was filling up. By 9:30a.m., I had wowed the audience and made an offer from stage to buy an advanced course and made 300 sales..!

Andy

P.S.: As a footnote, I took my new partner with me and now she is my wife and we have a beautiful family together.

Also, since speaking alongside Tony Robbins in London that day, I have spoken in Ireland, USA, Australia, Singapore, Malaysia, Dubai, South Africa, Poland, Belgium, Holland, Thailand and New Zealand. I've shared the stage with Sir Richard Branson (Virgin)

> *Donald Trump and Alan Sugar (The Apprentice), Robert Kiyosaki (Rich Dad Poor Dad), Sir Bob Geldof (Live Aid) Steve Wozniak (Apple Co-Founder) Jordan Belfort (The Wolf of Wall Street), Sebastian Coe (Olympic Champion), Brian Tracy, Bob Proctor, Dr John Demartini (The Secret), Les Brown, Paul McKenna, Nick Vujicic (the YouTube Phenomenon) George Foreman (World Heavyweight Boxing Champion), Erin Brockovich, Bill Cosby, Larry King, Steve Forbes (Forbes Magazine) and former President of the United States Bill Clinton."*

Since then, having worked all over the world, Andy is also a Number 1 Best Selling Author of the book *Passion into Profit: How to Make Big Money from who you are and what you know.*

Andy Harrington is the founder of the Public Speakers University and The Professional Speakers Academy, the world's leading speaker training program.

He has spoken alongside presidents, coached celebrities and industry leaders. He has spoken alongside some of the world's most amazing people as you can see above.

Check him out at www.andyharrington.com

What have we learnt from Andy's experience above? Persistence. We learnt about persistence. No matter the amount of obstacles Andy was persistent. We must have a passion for what we do or want to achieve. And if you want your customers to do business with you, you must show that real deep passion, and transfer that feeling into their hearts. No matter how much obstacles you face, keep that passion and push forward.

The late great Jim Rohn once said, *"If you really want to do something, you'll find a way. If you don't, you'll find an excuse."*

If you are in a position at this time where it's not the thing you want to be doing in your career, don't make any excuses or find any reason why you haven't found a way as yet. Start small by doing things you would enjoy and especially those things you can potentially turn into a career. Once you begin seeing results from those actions, let it encourage you to keep trying and moving forward.

You've already done a number of things in your meeting with your customer. Let's recap the summary of the meeting thus far.

As you can see on the next page, the summary of our entire conversation so far as brought us to this point. We've already met the customer and started the meeting.

To continue from this point forward, it is about time we begin developing a passion within the customer for what we have.

Sent e-mail/letter

Phone Call

- Introduce
- If it's a Bad time
- Reference to email/letter
- Interesting?
- Set meeting with two date options

Start meeting

- Greeting
- Grab Attention

Small Talk

Establish the Objective

- Customer's Benefit
- Agenda
- Anything to add – Continue?

But we are not selling at this point. Not yet at least.

In this chapter you would create a desire, the passion, a longing for your product or services before you even present it. You would build up so much value in the eyes of the customer that they would be craving to know what you have for them. That's how you transfer your passion over to them.

You will also learn to:

1. Be in control of conversation at all times.

2. Get necessary information from customer that would be vital to your success as well as the customer achieving their goals.

3. You'd help the customer uncover any issues or needs that they may have and resolve or meet those needs.

4. Position yourself as a solution finder or the one with an opportunity without saying that you have an opportunity.
5. You'd be able to show that you create much value.
6. Once you show that you create value, they would listen to you.

If you can successfully do this, you can close your new business prospects much faster. Also, after successfully doing this with new clients, when they continue doing business with you, they would not even need to go through the sales process with your communication techniques again because they would have so much trust and faith in you that you'd just have to make recommendations, and they would oblige.

> *"You'll never be any good if you*
> *don't know that you are"*

One thing I really admire is action. When a person wants to do something well and they are serious about it, they begin to take action. They are unconcerned with how many times they may make mistakes or fail, and they would push through until they succeed. The only way to know your skill level, the only way to know if you are any good, it to take action and see what results you are getting.

Up until this point, I hope you have started taking action on the various steps I have given to you and you observed how the people you use these techniques with, respond to you.

Let's move forward in this chapter.

After you've asked them "Is there anything you'd like to add before we begin/continue?" The client may or may not have anything to add in their response. In most instances, I've realised that most of the times, in that moment they would say "no, it's okay" so the meeting can begin.

If you want to get your customer engaged in you and what you have to offer, please note that as John C. Maxwell rightfully puts it, "*People do not care about how much you know until they know how much you care.*" Read that again. Underline it. Study It.

> "People do not care about how much you
> know, until they know how much you care"

In order for them to be interested in you, you need to be genuinely and sincerely interested in them.

THE PASSION PROCESS

To take the conversation to the next level after you've asked them to continue, it's a simple three step process. Is it easy to remember just three things again? I sure hope so.

This three-step process is vital to the success of your communication with the customer. If you do not do this and follow it as I say, you will definitely be perceived as a pushy salesperson because your pitch, tone and overall message would sound salesy. If you do it right, the customer would have no idea you're using simple communication techniques with them. You'd build a lot more rapport and they would feel comfortable knowing that you are genuinely seeking their interests.

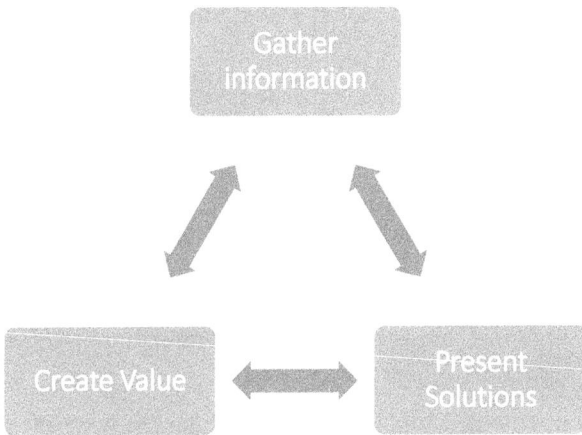

Take a look at the diagram presented. You'd see the three step process in building passion for what you have to offer simply laid out. Let me explain it to you in a bit more detail here. We need to take the conversation in the direction where we can get as much necessary information as possible that we can use to successfully help the customer while we achieve our goals in the process.

The information that you need to get from the customer would be their Needs and Wants. Of course, how difficult is it to just ask, *"what do you need?"* and *"what do you want?"* Usually they would just tell us! Simple right?

No. Many times, customers think they know what they want or need, or they have an idea. They may even be right about knowing what they want or need, but it is your job to make sure that you don't make a judgement and decision too quickly that can jeopardise the connection with that person.

You need to ask as many questions as you can and get the information from the customer. Do not prompt answers from your customer. Be direct and ask your questions in such a way that you get direct answers.

However, there is one really important thing that is vital information. This one thing is much more important than the customer's needs and wants. If you do not know what this is, it would be more difficult to get the business and close the sale. But if you do know it, then you'd be speaking to the person's emotions directly, and creating so much value and leaving such an impact on them, that no other people in your industry who they would interact with, would be able to do to them. This my friend would be an everlasting feeling and impression you'd leave with them. You need to ask questions, find out their needs, their wants and their emotional drive (the deep reason why they need their needs).

People won't tell you their emotional drive because many times they themselves don't know that they have one. No matter what you ask, they would not tell you. You have to 'discover' what it is. What really drives them? Is it a pull factor of something positive as an end result? Or is it a negative push factor that they want to get away from or get rid of?

Be mindful of the fact that it is very easy to confuse a need with an emotional drive. Remember Andy's story earlier in this chapter, I showed you how he was persistent? His persistence came about as a result of having passion for what he does, but behind all of that, he had an emotional drive. He had both push and pull factors. His push factor was to get out of the rut he was experiencing in 2009 because he was a grown man living in his mother's apartment. Secondly, he had a massive dream of speaking on the big stage because it would give him the fulfilment in life he desired.

If I had to sell something to him, I'd have to ask questions where I would try to understand why he really wants to get out of the rut and also, why he really wants to reach that peak in life. Once I know exactly why, I can speak directly to that emotion. That's discovering the emotional drive.

"Buyers want solutions and
new opportunities.

They do not buy because of what our products and services are.
They buy because of what our products and services can do."

I want you to do a brief exercise right now. Pretend you are with a customer asking a series of questions and you are getting the vital information you need from them. Let us fill in the spaces with the details you are discovering from the conversation you are having with them.

Write down points relating to your customer's responses under each heading

What is the purpose of their purchase?

....

....

....

....

....

What does your customer need (features, budget, timeline):

....

....

....

....

....

Any wants, other considerations, additional requests/preferences if possible:

....
....
....
....
....

Emotional reason behind purchase:

....
....
....
....
....

You should have an idea of what kind of information you require from the customer after this exercise. However, I want you to take a serious look at the emotional reason. This part is very important. Remember, do not confuse it with a need. It has to be something you discovered about them in the conversation that is the real reason why they would benefit.

Ernest Hemingway once said, "When people talk listen completely, most people never listen."

This part of the conversation where you have to get relevant information from the customer, you need to do as little amount of talking as possible. Yes, you need to talk less than you customer. The only and best way to do this is by asking questions.

Asking questions is the best way to control a conversation and direct the flow of the conversation to where you want it to go.

Usually I'm asked, "What kind of questions should I be asking?" It's not so much the kind of questions you ask but the way in which your questions flow that makes the impact. The best way to gather vital information from the customer, so you can discover their emotional drive is by asking them in a specific order.

Firstly, let's briefly take a look at what you must do in order to ask those questions:

1. Your questions needs to be in a conversational form. It should not be like an interview where the atmosphere is uncomfortable. Your customer needs to feel relaxed and feel as if those questions are because of your genuine interest in them.

2. They need to be phrased in such a way that it would create a sense of urgency in their minds as you go along asking them the questions. This would begin to create a gap in their minds and open their eyes to realise where they are presently vs where they'd want to be without you telling or showing them.

3. Then you need to widen that gap so that it would build their desire for what you have so much so, that they want it (even though you have not started selling them as yet or even mentioned what it is). E.g., *"what would happen if you don't get that?"*

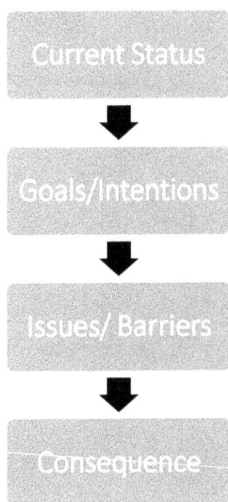

You must ask questions in this order.

There is not any limit to the amount of questions you can ask however, I do have some recommendations that I know works flawlessly in achieving the goal of getting the vital necessary information and discovering the emotional drive.

Remember, your passion here about yourself, what you represent and how you seek their interest opens doors for you.

After asking "Is there anything you'd like to add before we begin/continue?" You then move on to questioning the customer. When you ask a question, it firstly cuts any awkward silence that may potentially be present. But begin with questions about the current state of affairs of the customer that's in front of you.

Please do not ask, *"What's your current status?"* Only you understand what you mean by current status and not the customer. Current status to the customer could be interpreted to marital status and I do not think you'd want them to answer that. Be a bit more specific to the customer or their situation e.g., *"Tell me, how have your equipment been running in the last three months?"*

As they begin to answer that, you listen, and ask another relevant question pertaining to what they said. You can carry on from there for a while.

Note, you do not need to walk with questions prepared beforehand. You will _not_ have a proper flow and the conversation would be dis-jointed if you use or depend on them too much. You need to listen and respond accordingly.

Once you believe you have quite a good bit of information that is useful (take notes either mentally or written), then you move onto the second part about their goals or intentions and ask them questions in reference to where they would like to be or what they want to achieve, or where they see themselves. E.g., *"Where would you like to see the company in the next six months?"*

Already in their minds a gap is being created about where they are now versus where they want to be, and they begin to see this for themselves. Best part is, you're not telling them this. They're seeing it for themselves.

After they have shown you where they would like to be, and both of you can see that gap in your minds, you move on to the third part of the questioning smoothly and here you can ask just one question; *"What's keeping you back from achieving that goal now?"*

They would tell you. You will then understand what held them back to this point. Here, the customer begins to see what's stopping them within the gap.

What I recommend you do now is that you try to make things worse for them (in their head that is). Let them taste fear a bit without you prompting them. This is where we move on to the consequence question which is having them realise what would be the consequences of their present action/ inaction of not making the right choice/s. For example, *"What would happen if you do not achieve that goal at all?"*

If you notice something, each category is related to each other.

- The goals question/s is related to the current status to establish the gap.
- The issues/ barriers is related to the goals question to understand the gap.
- The consequence question is related to the goals to create the urgency and panic of not achieving the goal. This opens their eyes to what's missing at this point.

Do you see how the flow of questions are important? Did you notice that I left the consequence questions as the last because people remember or respond mostly to the last thing that they experience. Here you are keeping them in a state of mind where they now want to make a change.

Did we sell anything as yet? – **No.**
Does the situation make them want what we have? – **Yes.**

You do a number of other things when you ask the questions in this way:

1. It makes you come across as very knowledgeable in the customer's eyes.
2. You hold power of the conversation without forcing a customer to purchase.
3. You make them intrigued by you and want to do business with you.
4. You are seeking their interests and they feel a connection with you.

Here are just some examples of questions from each category. You can use your own one if you do not see any below that would be suitable for you to use. If that is the case, please write it down in this book.

Current Status

How is the recent _____ affecting your operations?
How much did you plan to invest?
What are your looking for?

When would you want this?

Who are your current suppliers? How did you select them?

Where are you seeing success with this present process?

When do you want this?

How is your current transport situation?

Goals/Intentions

In addition to this _____ what do you plan to achieve in the near future?

How would you like your clients or business associates see you when you approach them?

What would you like your staff doing differently?

What changes would you like to see?

What other factors are important to the development of the business?

Where would you like to be six months from now? A year?

What are your objectives for the next two months?

Can you describe what you would want your operations to look like at maximum performance?

Issues/Barriers

What time constraints are you facing right now?

What obstacles are you facing at present that would prevent you from moving forward?

What is keeping you back from achieving this now?

What specific actions/events needs to take place before moving forward?

Consequence

What would happen if you don't achieve that goal?

What would achieving the outcome allow you to do?

What would happen when you are able to _____?

How will your team perform differently?

What would be the outcome if _____?

PRESENT SOLUTION

"Most people do not listen with the intent to understand; they listen with the intent to reply."

~Stephen R. Covey

After you have successfully questioned the customer in a comfortable conversational way, based on the information that was given to you and all that was said, you can make a transition to providing a solution.

Now providing the solution is made up of three parts. Is it easy to remember three things?

Show that you understand them. Your statement in providing a solution would consist of:

1. Solution (type of product or service).
2. Benefit (relating to customer needs/wants).
3. Appeal to emotional reason behind purchase.

Sent Email/Letter

Phone Call

- Introduce
- If it's a Bad time
- Reference to email/letter
- Interesting?
- Set meeting – 2 date options

Start meeting

- Greeting
- Grab Attention

Small Talk

Establish the Objective

- Customer's Benefit
- Agenda
- Anything to add – Continue?

Questions

- Current Status
- Goals/Intentions
- Issues/Barriers
- Consequence

Provide the Solution

- Solution
- Benefits
- Appeal to Emotional Drive

E.g., *based on what you have just told me, I recommend 'Solution A' because it will give you 'Benefit 1' and 'Benefit 2' which you have said are critical to your overall operations. The money and time (emotional drive) and reduced labour saved will help take your company to the top in your region and industry (emotional drive).*

Look at the structure of that statement again. Look at the timing in which it is used in the sales process as per the column on the left.

It takes into account that you have listened well to your customer when you were asking them the questions in a conversational manner. As a result, the customer would already feel comfortable and respect your decision in providing a solution (product or service or both).

Let's break down the statement a bit further.

'Based on what you have just told me'. The customer cannot disagree with you because you are confirming that you are using information that they just provided you with.

Recommending Solution A: The customer would have a positive feeling about your recommendation because it is coming from a place of authority and expertise. You do not 'think', you are not 'suggesting', you are making a recommendation.

Then, you state two main benefits that are applicable to the customer and or their situation. I recommend using two because it is easy to explain to the customer and you won't confuse yourself in the process. But these benefits would act as the solution to their problems or the new opportunity that they would need.

Ending the statement with an appeal to the emotional drive behind the reason the customer would need your product or service leaves a lasting impression on them because people tend to remember the most as well as respond (verbally or non-verbally) to the last thing that was said to them. This way, you'd have the most amount of impact and power in what you are selling which would positively influence them.

Take note of this, nowhere in the statement did I use 'me', 'I' or 'my' because it would become too salesy and the customer would subconsciously feel like you are trying to sell them. At that point, they can pull up their 'bullshit' screen and block any future suggestions coming from you. Using 'you' as much as you can where necessary, is more customer centric and give them a feeling that you are genuine.

The structure of your statement is important in having them keep their guards down against the phobia of the salesman.

CREATE VALUE

Creating value comes as part of your solution presented. If you look at the structure of the statement again:

"Based on what you have just told me, I recommend 'Solution A' because it will give you 'Benefit 1' and 'Benefit 2' which you have said are critical to your overall operations. The money and time (emotional drive) and reduced labour saved will help take your company to the top in your region and industry (emotional drive)."

You will notice I have placed the two benefits with a short reason and I appealed to the emotional reason.

Giving a valid reason 'why' when you make your recommendation is adding significant value to your solution provided, as well as widening the gap in the process. Here, your solution gap is so wide that the desire built up is strong. Your customer would be feeling like – *"I've got to have this now!"*

SUMMARY

- Develop a passion in the hearts and minds of the people you are talking to.
- Use questions to control conversations and direct the conversation wherever you want it to go.
- Ask questions in a particular order of current status or what's happening now, goals or intentions of where the person wants to be. Then what has delayed the goals from happening now and what would happen if the goal is not achieved.
- Listen for more than just the needs and wants.
- Try to listen for and discover what the emotional drive of the person is.
- Provide a solution relevant to each customer.
- Use the words 'I recommend' to speak from a position of authority.
- Always appeal to the emotional reason at the end.
- Make sure you create a gap in the minds and hearts of the customer.
- Widen those gaps to strengthen the desire of the customer.
- Speak to the customer using 'you' instead of 'I', 'me', 'we', 'our'.

Go practice with someone. Go interact with real customers and see for yourself how it works.

CHAPTER 5

OVERCOMING OBJECTIONS AND OBSTACLES

"One important key to Success is
Self-Confidence. An important key to
Self-Confidence is preparation."
~Romeo Effs

In life we all face great challenges. I'm sure you have faced many up until this point. I am also very sure you have overcome many of them as well! So if it is possible for us to look back and say, 'I have grown, I have overcome it' then I am sure that no matter what you are going through right now that seems to be a challenge in your life, you will soon add that to the list of things that you have overcome and grown from.

By the end of this chapter, you will learn certain techniques that would help you to overcome any objection a client gives to you. Especially the ones that involves the cost of your products or services. I have used my experience in many years of sales (and I still sell to get companies to 'buy in' on my Corporate Training courses), and the one thing that I do is that I train people 'not to give discounts' unless it is absolutely necessary to close a sale. Why sell low when you can sell high, by using effective communication techniques?

Here I have an experience I want to share with you. Romeo is a good friend of mine who I must say was one of the major reasons behind me writing this book. He is an author and Entrepreneur. Romeo and I first met in 2014 when I went to one of Andy Harrington's professional speaking three-day university boot camp in London. We have since always kept in touch. One day he came to Trinidad on business and on one of the occasions we were hanging out, I expressed to him my desire to write a book. Through his encouragement and help, the rest his history. Read what Romeo has to say about his experiences in overcoming obstacles and objections:

"Adrian, this story relates to a time in my life, back in 2013, when I had the most senior position that I've had in the corporate world. I was a senior exec in the UK for a

FTSE 250 company earning a very good salary earning about 200,000.00 a year, managing a P and L of close to about 900million. Of course reporting directly to the CEO of that business. Prior to that I was employed with the business as their group Supply Chain Manager. Within six months, I was able to get promoted to the position of the Group Director of Projects (which is a major position in the organisation).

Being the only person of colour within the directorship, and with my CEO who was also of an Indian decent, there were quite a lot of upheavals or barriers that I needed to overcome because there was constant push-back and rejection from the senior management on certain things. This was in 2011. In 2013 I was actually in one of the locations for a meeting, because I had a team count of close to maybe 20, and I was having a meeting with some of my team. One of the particular board members actually approached me and asked if we could have a meeting. In the moment, I kind of figured that 'something was up' because this was one of the board members who frankly, was very objective to me being in the position that I was at, and was pushing back hard on a lot of things that I would recommend. As I walked into the meeting room, the first thing I said to him was,

"Okay, tell me what the package is?"

He pretty much said to me, "What do you mean what the package is?"

I said, "Look, I know the reason you're here is to fire me so just tell me what the package is?"

He replied, "You're a seasoned player aren't you?"

"Yes I am, I've been doing this thing for a long time. I know what to expect,"

Of course he didn't 'beat around the bush', he told me what the package was. I was shipped off even though they took me through the whole mandatory consultative period of I think about 30 days trying to see if they could relocate me somewhere in the business etc. I knew that they were just playing the whole legal game where that was concerned. After the 30 days I was sent on leave for about six months.

This was a really, really tough blow for me personally because not only that I feel I was decapitated by the fact that I was made redundant from the most senior role that I've had in my corporate career, I also had done a lot of work for this organisation. My work had won several awards for the business. My work had even gotten the business through a lot of doors and helped it to win a lot of contracts. I was feeling very hurt that the business could have actually taken that decision.

To be totally candid as well, I was also hurting from the fact that I had lost a status of who I was in the corporate world. I went home and went through a state of a kind of 'personal depression' which was really very hard. I kind of then had to deal with fighting with the demons from within. I had to deal with the whole notion of not blaming myself because that's what I was doing. I had to deal with the notion of realising that to overcome this objection that this was not the end of the road for me because I was still very qualified, I was still Romeo, I still had gained a lot of experience and a lot of knowledge from this job and all the other jobs that I've had. Then I just started re-evaluating and thinking, 'Okay, time to get out of the pit, what's the next move?'

The next move that I decided to do was to actually go after my ultimate vision and my ultimate dream which was really to start my own business. I then had to decide on the route I was going to go in terms of doing that. Of course there were challenges. There were challenges of 'How do I finance the business?' There were challenges around putting together the right strategy, putting together the right team and it was through the whole notion of first dealing with overcoming the barriers that I placed on myself! Personally overcoming that! Once I was able to deal with that, and to overcome that, then I was able to step out and start reaching out for help and then start asking people within my network for their help in terms of their connections, in terms of their knowledge base etc., I could get the business up and running and start it.

Since I've started the business, we've had to deal with things like any start up. There are lots of other obstacles that's going to come in your way. The obstacle of 'How do you actually acquire clients?' and when a client says "No" 'what do you do?' How do you deal with the whole notion of when you're pitching for finance and an investor turns you down, how do you overcome that? I had to personally overcome all of those situations! I ended up pitching about twenty times before an investor said to me 'yes' they would invest in the business. But I didn't give up!

I think it's mainly because I dealt with the internal demons that I had, thinking 'How dare someone says no to me?' How dare someone say no to this person who is so qualified and so experienced? I had to deal with that and know that:

It's not personal.

The other persons have their own baggage and their own stuff they're dealing with.

You don't know what that person is dealing with at the time, or why they are going to object to either invest or to listen to you, or to say 'yes'. I had to learn that, no matter how many times I hear 'no', no matter how many times the door was shut, no matter how many times I was shoved out I had to learn that I just had to pick myself up and I had to just keep going. I had to just keep asking, I had to just keep pushing because, that's the only way you're going to make progress. That's the only way you're going to be able to achieve the success that you really want to achieve in anything that you do!

Romeo is the CEO of Aspyre Group and Founder of the Empire Builders, an entrepreneur, former C-Suite Executive and high performance coach and mentor to CEO's globally, author and international speaker.

He specialises in Business Strategy and is known for being a Business Gladiator and Fixer who solves problems, manage crisis and save reputations.

Check him out at www.romeoeffs.com

Would it be fair for me to say that Romeo's experience has given us some insight into some of the obstacles that he faced? Would it also make sense to say that some of those obstacles were very serious in nature, and in life there are many people who have similar challenges and are struggling to deal with it? Would you agree then that Romeo used his obstacles as a platform to take him to the next level?

Think about the many challenges you've faced in the past and how you've overcome them and grown from them. It may be fair to say that right now you are facing a major challenge or obstacle in your life and it's probably giving you hell. But do you agree that one day you are going to look back at it knowing that you overcame it?

That's how we are going to look at objections in the sales process. It isn't actually anything big to be fearful about but something that we should embrace as part of life just as any other obstacle we've overcome. Let's focus in on this a little more. In the sales process how do we really define the objection?

An objection in the sales process is really a form of rejection where there is a reason, or string of reasons that may appear from the customer to delay or stop the sale. They're basically saying, *"I do not want to spend any money as yet."*

This is a serious feeling for a customer to have because not only is it possible for them to think that, but it is also a major deterrent for salespeople or business owners to pursue their goals. People hate rejection. People hate being rejected. After all the work you've put in, into selling the customer and creating value in the end where you really emphasise that emotional reason it's really hard to hear a customer say "no". It's hard to hear a spouse say "no". It's hard to hear a boss say "no".

Sent Email/Letter

Phone Call

- Introduce
- If it's a Bad time
- Reference to email/letter
- Interesting?
- Set meeting – 2 date options

Start meeting

- Greeting
- Grab Attention

Small Talk

Establish the Objective

- Customer's Benefit
- Agenda
- Anything to add – Continue?

Questions

- Current Status
- Goals/Intentions
- Issues/Barriers
- Consequence

Provide the Solution

- Solution
- Benefits
- Appeal to Emotional Drive

Closing Question

Would Romeo reach where he is today if he stopped when he faced those obstacles or objections of life? Would Andy Harrington be the world's number one speaker if he had left the arena or decided not to speak when he saw empty seats the first time he stepped out onto the stage? As Og Mandino rightfully put in his book *The Greatest Salesman in the World*, "*I will persist until I succeed*".

Looking at the summary on the left, let us begin to understand what we need to do in order to rid ourselves mentally and emotionally of the potential 'fear of rejection' that may loom over our heads.

How do many sales people react to objections? They fall into a defence mode, and begin to think and feel and act in a way that their 'product is better'. Don't find your state of mind there. In fact, understanding what is stopping your potential client from making a decision in your favour is the best way to come closer to closing any sale where there is an objection. Once you know why he or she is hesitating, you can reply directly to that specific objection.

To overcome feelings of failure, you must remain intensely focused on the end results, not the obstacles set down before you. There is an easy way to help you do this.

When providing a solution or a new opportunity to a buyer/customer, you may in most cases encounter obstacles, barriers or objections when that solution is provided. As a professional, you need to develop solutions unique to each buyer. A professional sales person or business person negotiates and meets the hidden needs of customer. How do we now do this?

You've got to mentally prep yourself for the next step by asking a question! Yes! Ask a question! But not with a random unrelated question. There needs to be a flow that suits the conversation as well as sets you up to respond and resolve any objections that would possibly appear (if the customer has one and is not sold at this point).

After you provide the solution with the statement beginning with, "Based on what you have just told me…" Before the customer even reply's to your recommendation, after you've stated their emotional reason, you need to ask a closing question.

A closing question is a specifically designed question where the response that is required needs to be a confirmation of what you recommended as either, *"yes, I agree and I want that"* or *"no, I do not want that"*. But in most cases, the customer is going to think "yes".

You would have already put the customer into a buying frame of mind. In fact you'd put them into that frame of mind so strongly that they are ready to do something so profound that salespeople either fear it or get excited about it.

Before we proceed to deal with the customer's response, let's break down this 'closing question'.

The closing question can come in three forms. Remember, that all you need to look out for is a confirmation from the customer of yes or no. But it does not have to be verbal. It can be non-verbal like a headshake.

- How does this look?
- Does this sound like what you're looking for?
- What are your thoughts?

"Based on what you have just told me, I recommend 'Solution A' because it will give you 'Benefit 1' and 'Benefit 2' which you have said are critical to your overall operations. The money and time (emotional drive) and reduced labour saved, will help take your company to the top in your region and industry (emotional drive)."

"How does this look? Or does this sound like what you're looking for? Or what are your thoughts?"

The customer is at this point either going to indicate their willingness to proceed with the purchase, or they're going to give you an objection. But you'd be ready. Both mentally and emotionally for whatever their response is going to be.

A good thing about the closing question is that it can be used any time after solution is presented, even if it is needed more than once.

THE COMMONLY USED OBJECTIONS

In a world where value on almost anything is determined by a financial amount I would like to address in full detail in this chapter, how to overcome the 'price objection'.

1. Price Objection

"Your price is too high!" **or** *"It is too expensive!"* **or** *"I can get it cheaper somewhere else!"*

Have you ever heard something like that before? Sounds familiar? What do you do in moments when a customer gives you that response?

Let me share with you my experience from over the years of how you separate the amateurs from the professional influencers. From this you would determine if your skills need upgrading or if you're already a pro!

The amateurs who find it difficult to overcome this objection does something that turns their customer off. And they don't even realise that they're doing it. When they receive the objection that 'your price is too high', people immediately try to resolve the objection. Or at least they try to. What happens is a series of hesitation and nervousness. For instance;

Customer: *"I think your price is too high."*

Salesman: *"Okay, well you know, we (or our product) have* (this feature and that feature …)."

Does this sound familiar to you? Have you ever been in a position where you were the buyer and when you expressed your feelings about the price being high or expensive, did the person who was selling to you begin to defend their product or service by stating all the facts, features and benefits, with more excitement? Did they even try to make their competitor look 'bad'?

If you can think of such an experience and say to yourself *"yes I am familiar with that"*, then you surely know how it feels to be bombarded by information you are not interested in.

Here's why this happens a lot. Many sales people or even small business owners who have not received any formal sales training tend to jump into a 'defence mode' about their products or service so that they can defend its value or, the price that they offer. The thing is, that with so many people who do that, customers no longer buy into the idea that what you are saying adds any additional value. Sometimes, customers raise this objection just as an excuse so that they won't have to buy from you.

Customers have the ability to read through bullshit. No longer do we live in a world where, the more you tell someone about the great things your product has, they are convinced. They need to see value. More specifically, they need to see how it is valuable to them.

After you've asked all the appropriate questions, got all the necessary information about their needs, wants and figured out their emotional reason behind buying anything, and they object to the price, you need to respond to the objection like a professional. Like someone who is speaking from the position of authority. Like the authority that made a significant recommendation and can ensure the customer that they are making the right decision.

Don't hesitate when they object to the price, and neither should you defend yourself and jump into calling out all the features, functions and benefits. When you do that you do that from a position of high emotions. You are acting on how you feel and not from a position of 'common sense'. Step back for a second and respond in a way that instead of you being in the hot seat of having to answer to the customer as to why your price is so high, you need to get out of the 'hot seat' and put the customer there in the blink of an eye. Why stress yourself out in the hot seat of high emotions that would make you react? Handle it like this;

Customer: *"I think your price is too high."*

Salesman: *"I appreciate what you're saying but, why do you think the price is too high?"*

Do you see what happens there?

Do you know what you just did for yourself and to the customer?

As Blair Singer, the author of *Little Voice Mastery* puts it, you have to acknowledge the objection and ask a question.

The psychological game you just played by acknowledging the objection and asking the question has a huge impact on how positive the potential result of closing the sale would be. What you would have done by taking this action is that you took yourself out of the 'hot seat' and placed the customer into it. You also do not have to defend yourself and neither do you have to speak from an area of high emotions.

In fact, you also open the forum to identify if the objection was a true objection that the customer really thinks your price is high (because they would give you a reason). If there is no reason or they are really hesitating to give an answer, chances are they were just bluffing to see if you would give them a discount or they just do not want to buy.

I do not like giving discounts unless I want to. I recommend you do the same. Why under value your products or services for less money and the same amount of effort. If you can show you provide great value, wouldn't you like to get the maximum financial value from it?

Let's assume the customer at this point either wanted to get a discount or really just thought that the price was too high.

How do we deal with this? Well, I am going to show you a formula that I used for many years that helped me closed so many deals in my days of sales at BMW. This formula has helped me in the top three sales people in the country. It also helped in many other business deals and has helped many people who learnt it in my trainings, to close more deals with no discounts.

If you can practice this formula, and if you can use this from today on someone, you would immediately see results. If you do not use this, you could possibly stay in the same position. Look at this:

Customer: *"I think your price is too high."*

Salesman: *"I appreciate what you're saying but, why do you think the price is too high?"*

Please note, use the same words the customer uses as underlined above. If the customer says *"I'm getting it cheaper elsewhere"* respond by asking, *"I appreciate what you're saying but why do you think you're getting it cheaper elsewhere?"* Or *"It's too expensive"* *"I appreciate what you're saying but why do you think it's too expensive?"*

What you do by repeating their words is that you show them you are listening to them and you are genuinely interested in them and their needs. They wouldn't feel like you're throwing them into the hot seat (but in fact you are). They would instead feel good about you and begin to think that you want to help them (which you do).

Let's say the customer responds with a reason for it being high;

Customer: *"I think your price is too high."*

Salesman: *"I appreciate what you're saying but, why do you think the price is too high?"*

Customer: *"Well, I'm getting it cheaper at XYZ company."*

Sent Email/Letter

Phone Call

- Introduce
- If it's a Bad time
- Reference to email/letter
- Interesting?
- Set meeting – 2 date options

Start meeting

- Greeting
- Grab Attention

Small Talk

Establish the Objective

- Customer's Benefit
- Agenda
- Anything to add – Continue?

Questions

- Current Status
- Goals/Intentions
- Issues/Barriers
- Consequence

Provide the Solution

- Solution
- Benefits
- Appeal to Emotional Drive

Closing Question

Objection (Optional if there is one)

- Acknowledge Objection

Salesman: *"Okay, what price are they giving you?" (This is another question to control the conversation. The customer can either tell you or not. It is up to them).*

If the customer tells you a price or even if they don't want to. Or, there was a different reason and excuse your next response in building value to get the customer to buy, would be to go straight into the formula like this:

Salesman: *"Okay, let's take a closer look."*

Those words underlined there are very important because it make the customer's ears perk up and listen to what you have to say.

Looking to the left you will see I have added below the process we worked on in the last couple pages.

Let us continue now to work on this strategy that takes the customer into the buying frame of mind.

At this point you will need a pen and paper to continue this conversation with the customer. It is a lot more difficult to do this verbally. It is much easier for both you and the customer because you would be using more senses. The senses of sight, sound and touch. By using more senses to have this part of the conversation, it is more memorable, and the feeling you would give the customer would also be memorable even if they do not remember the facts. The best part of that is, people buy based on how they feel. People buy on emotions.

Get your pen and paper out and start following the explanation I am going to give you exactly as I give you. The order of this explanation is very important. If you do not explain this in the order that I show you, you can actually make this formula work against you and have the customer more confused than before. Let's do this right. Let's practice this right. There would be about eight steps. You must do it in sequential order.

Please note, nowhere else is this formula documented. This book is the first time I am publicly showing this formula. Hold this close to you, near to you and dear to you. Practice it and influence much more people to do business with you.

The first thing I want you to do is draw the following chart below for your customer, after you say, *"let's take a closer look"*.

Show the customer the layout of what you're going to do. It's a little bit of mathematics but it is very simple. The order or flow of the information presented would make it easy.

Step one would be to start labelling to show the customer this is where you are going and set the tone for an open mind from them.

Firstly you are going to lay out what you are selling or your company (top left side) and the competition or their product (top right side). If you do not have a direct competitor to use from the customer's information, do not put the word 'competition' but in fact use 'industry'. Then you would place the product or service to the top middle to indicate that this is what we are discussing. Then you would include the prices. If you do not have the competition's prices you can put the industry's average price.

This is step one!

Product (e.g. Power Drill)

($1,000.00) My Product/Company (e.g. ABC)	($900.00) Competitor/ Product/ Industry (e.g. Industry)

Please take note, this works best if your price is more expensive than the competition or, it's too high and you need to compare it to the industry. If your price is lower, there is no need to justify your price, because it's understood that you have more value.

Step two is to list what features of your product and or service (or both), that are similar between you and the competition or industry (use the middle in the above table). By doing this you show that you do not speak ill of your competition or industry but that they too have value that you also acknowledge. People respect those who respect others.

Only list about three-five things. Nothing more. Usually I use the best four. This makes the explanation very simple, and easy to understand.

Step three is to begin listing up to three things that you have of which is unique to your product, service and company. It does not have to be directly related to your product as you can show or add value to your product or services by listing what's unique to you.

Product (e.g., power drill)

Titles (1)	($1,000.00) My Product/ Company (e.g. ABC)	($900.00) Competitor/ Product/ Industry (e.g. Industry)
Similar Features (2)	Heavy Duty Hammer Function Portable Strong Brand	Heavy Duty Hammer Function Portable Strong Brand
Unique To us (3)	Extended Warranty Spare Parts Trained Staff (Handle issues)	XXX XXX XXX

Before I continue with the necessary steps, can you see how simple everything about your product/service (using the example of the power drill above) is laid out for both you and the customer?

You have a lot of information right there. But remember, you need to continue following the order of how you are supposed to present this information. Step one is listing out the titles of the things you would discuss. Then step two is only listing what is similar between your offering and the competition or industry. Thirdly, only list what is unique to you that the competition or industry would not have (not necessarily direct features of the product in question but unique services that you also offer that would come with purchasing from you).

It is important when you reach step three, that you do not say the words *"if you buy from us"* or, *"what we have"* because you do not want to appear 'cocky' in your explanation nor do you want to be self-focused. Better to say *"what you'd get that's unique is…."* Then you begin to list each one out.

Now it is a must that everything you write, EVERY word that you put on that piece of paper, you say it as you write it so the customer can follow. Do not write, and list everything, and then decide to explain it to your customer after you wrote it. That would confuse them. The human brain would understand faster and easier if you explain what you're writing *while* you're writing it. You need to explain it as you go along. This is the best strategy to overcoming the price objection.

Step four is very important. It is important because, your intro line to move to that step needs to be said correctly. In fact, you need to say it correctly in order for the customer to understand why you are doing what you are about to do. So, show the customer all the information that is laid out in front of them and then say these exact words:

Salesman: *"Now if I were to put a dollar value to each one of these."*

Immediately, you eliminate any question or concern the customer may have about you placing prices on what you've written.

> *Salesman: "Now if I were to put a dollar value to each one of these things/features...Let's say, as its heavy duty, which should cost $250.00." (write that in).*
>
> *"The hammer function, let's say that costs $350.00" (write that in also).*
>
> *"It's portable, so let's put $100.00" (write it in).*
>
> *"And it's a strong brand, so let's put $200.00" (write it in).*

Product (e.g. power drill)

Titles (1)	($1,000.00) My Product/ Company (e.g. ABC)	($900.00) Competitor/ Product/ Industry (e.g. Industry)	
Similar Features (2)	Heavy Duty Hammer Function Portable Strong Brand	Heavy Duty Hammer Function Portable Strong Brand	$250.00 $350.00 $100.00 $200.00
Unique To us (3)	Extended Warranty Spare Parts Trained Staff (Handle issues)	XXX XXX XXX	

You just laid out the value of the drill. The price adds up to what your competitor has it priced at or what the 'industry' should have it priced at. *Make sure that when you're putting prices for 'similar features' they total the cost of the competition's pricing e.g., in this case $900.00.*

We do not explain at this point that it adds up to the $900. You do not need to even tell the customer that. They would have been adding it up in their minds while you were writing the prices in.

You're probably wondering how I know the cost of individual features of the drill right? Well, I do not know the exact costs. This exercise is to put *'realistic economic value'* to features. Although the prices of the individual features are not accurate, they are realistic because they add up to the total of the $900.00 in this example. Basically, you come up with costs on the spot but ensure that you will total the similar features to that of the competition's (or industry's) pricing. Use easy numbers like I did here so it would be simple for both you and the customer to add e.g. $200.00, $350.00 etc.

By continuing without showing the customer that your total at this point is $900.00 (because most likely they've figured that out) you will see that a difference of $100.00 remains to reach our present price point of $1000.00. Let us continue with the flow.

Salesman: *"What about extended warranty? Let's put $150.00."*

"Spare parts availability? Let's put $100.00."

"We do invest in training staff to assist you with anything that you need. So how about $150.00?"

Product (e.g. power drill)

Titles (1)	($1,000.00) My Product/ Company (e.g. ABC)	($900.00) Competitor/ Product/ Industry (e.g. Industry)	
Similar Features (2)	Heavy Duty	Heavy Duty	$250.00
	Hammer Function	Hammer Function	$350.00
	Portable	Portable	$100.00
	Strong Brand	Strong Brand	$200.00
Unique To us (3)	Extended Warranty	XXX	**$150.00**
	Spare Parts	XXX	**$100.00**
	Trained Staff (Handle issues)	XXX	**$150.00**

At this point, the customer may either be sold, or intensively listening because you're making a damn good point. They've probably already totalled the cost in their heads by now. Here's how you are going to continue this price justification explanation:

Salesman: "As you see, in order to get everything listed here at (the competition's name/ or in the industry), you would have to pay $1,300.00" (write that total in after you say that line).

Product (e.g. power drill)

Titles (1)	($1,000.00) My Product/ Company (e.g. ABC)	($900.00) Competitor/ Product/ Industry (e.g. Industry)	
Similar Features (2)	Heavy Duty Hammer Function Portable Strong Brand	Heavy Duty Hammer Function Portable Strong Brand	$250.00 $350.00 $100.00 $200.00
Unique To us (3)	Extended Warranty Spare Parts Trained Staff (Handle issues)	XXX XXX XXX	$150.00 $100.00 $150.00
			$1300.00

At this point, if you've done everything correctly and in the order of which I just showed you, the customer would be in total agreement with you. Continue 'milking' this opportunity by putting the icing on the cake and wrap up your explanation saying these things:

Salesman: *"As you can see, in order to get <u>everything</u> listed here at (the competition's name/ or in the industry), you would have to pay $1,300.00."*

Draw an arrow from the $1,300.00 around the right side of the chart up to your pricing point and ask this question while you draw the arrow, *"Wouldn't you like to save $300.00?"*

$300.00 Product (e.g. power drill)

Titles (1)	($1,000.00) My Product/ Company (e.g. ABC)	($900.00) Competitor/ Product/ Industry (e.g. Industry)	
Similar **Features (2)**	Heavy Duty Hammer Function Portable Strong Brand	Heavy Duty Hammer Function Portable Strong Brand	$250.00 $350.00 $100.00 $200.00
Unique **To us (3)**	Extended Warranty Spare Parts Trained Staff (Handle issues)	XXX XXX XXX	$150.00 $100.00 $150.00
			$1300.00

Salesman: *"Wouldn't you like to save $300.00?"*

- *How does this look?*
- *Does this sound like what you're looking for?*
- *What are your thoughts?*

Use any one or two of the closing questions to end your explanation so the customer can now speak and give you their thoughts.

I have sold many, many things using this formula. This explanation. This price justification formula. I have closed many, many deals and won many big sales with this. I have overcome many, many price objections using this explanation. By closing with that question of how much money someone would like to save shifts their focus from what they're spending, to what they're saving.

At this point, you have just made this person crave your product or service. You just changed their feelings and played with their emotions so much that there is no question that you bring significant value to them.

Also, I have even overcome other types of objections using this formula even though it wasn't a price objection. Surprisingly it worked, but you need to be sure you can use it with your customer.

Two things can happen here based on how the customer responds: you will know if you can go in for that close; or if there is still hesitation on the decision to purchase.

I want you to get a scrap paper and practice that formula I just explained for you. Get it right, get a friend or colleague and explain it to them until they feel convinced. Use the next couple of lines to draw it out while you explain it to your colleague. Use different products and different prices. Remember, this one key point, when you're coming up with your final total of the more expensive price e.g., the $1,300.00 in the illustration above, an average of 20% or more is usually a good 'realistic' amount of showing how much more their cost would be if they were to purchase the item elsewhere.

……………………………………………………………..
……………………………………………………………...
……………………………………………………………...
……………………………………………………………...
……………………………………………………………...
……………………………………………………………...
……………………………………………………………...
……………………………………………………………...
……………………………………………………………...
……………………………………………………………...
……………………………………………………………...
……………………………………………………………...
……………………………………………………………...
……………………………………………………………...
……………………………………………………………...

Well done. You have just stepped up in your game of overcoming the price objection.

Let's say the customer is convinced. Just go in for a close. The chapter on closing strategies is next so you can see different ways, and know how to adapt. Based on your customer and experience in the conversation with them, which of the closing strategies would be the best to use.

But, if the customer seems to be hesitating, then there is something deeper that is going on. Something bigger and more important.

THE HIDDEN OBJECTION

In any sales course you do, they would call this hesitation a 'hidden objection' because it's an objection that was not revealed in the first place.

Now a hidden objection can appear for different reasons:

1. The customer did not want to tell you they do not want to buy, and used price as the 'go-to' objection.
2. The customer does not know that they even had a hidden objection that would keep them from making a decision and just thought that getting a good price should help them decide.
3. The customer was using it as a bluff in order to see if you can give them a better deal (as anyone would always like to get a deal).

How do you deal with a hidden objection when dealing with a customer?

Do you repeat the benefits of the product or service? The benefits of working with you? Unfortunately, too many sales people or business people do this. They repeat everything perhaps with more enthusiasm thinking that it would affect buying behaviour. No. It doesn't. You need to deal with a hidden objection directly. As Robert Keith Leavit says, 'People don't ask for facts in making up their minds. They would rather have one good, soul-satisfying emotion than a dozen facts". You need to be able to throw the original objection out the window and deal with this new one.

If you realise you cannot proceed with an agreement to close the sale and there is a hidden objection, you need to probe further and ask questions again. Test to see if you are meeting the needs of the customer.

Salesman: *"Are there any other concerns you may have at this time? What would keep you from making this decision now?"*

Once the customer identifies that objection that's keeping them from making their decision now, you need to throw the original objection out the window by saying *"I believe that the real concern isn't that you (original objection). But that this (hidden objection) is what is needed to proceed…is this so? In that case, once I can meet this need of yours, would you be able to proceed?"* They must say yes at this point. Here, you'd know if you can close that sale now or later on.

Let us look at other types of objections you would mostly encounter and look at how to deal with them quickly. Once you are familiar with them, you'd know how to deal with that objection and overcome any of the hidden objections that may arise.

Make sure and acknowledge all objections that come up. It would show that you listened before responding.

Complacency-: *Example: "I'm okay with the way things work right now."*

When complacency is the culprit, use a touch of fear to get the client to see why they need to make a decision and get them to start thinking about making the change.

Hopefully you would have researched the competition, because if you can show the client how their competitors made changes in their businesses they would begin to think hard. Nothing like a look at everything your competitors are doing that you are not, to move you to action.

Fear of Change-: *Example: "I don't want to change the way we've been doing things for 15 years. Too much can go wrong."*

Often related to complacency, fear of change makes the decision-making process a difficult one for many business owners. To overcome this objection, demonstrate past examples of change and how it was positive in that customer's industry. For instance, the different ways the industry has changed over the past 10 to 15 years and how the potential customer has adapted. It helps them to be less fearful and more confident about changing things up.

Trust-:*Example: "It seems like you know what you're doing, but how do I know you really have the necessary experience to do this?"*

Now trust takes time to build and if it is a hurdle for your potential client, you need to be honest and consistent across the board. Be forthcoming with information, share testimonials, case studies and references that takes away some of the uncertainty and give the client confidence in your ability to get the job done

Personal Politics-: *Example: "I told my brother's friend's wife, I'd use her company for my next project."*

Acknowledge this objection sincerely here. Sometimes there's not much you can do to usurp a family connection, but you can try to position yourself to be the next in line.

If this is an objection you're hearing from a potential client, think a few steps ahead and show the client what you can do in phase two of the project for instance.

External input-: *Example: "I need to run this by my wife/business partner/mentor before I do anything else."*

This is one of my favourites because this can often have a positive outcome, assuming the customer isn't using it as an excuse.

One way to make sure it doesn't end up as a deal-ending sales objection is to attempt to stay in the process. Try suggesting a joint sales meeting (which I always do) between the client and their counterparts to answer any questions, that would help facilitate their decision.

<u>Timing</u>-: *Example: "It's too much for me to take on right now; I'm too busy; Call me again in 6 months."*

If time management or lack of time is an issue for the client right now, chances are it will still be an issue in six months or a year. Make the decision to hire you, an easy one. Start by listing all of the benefits of working with you, outline value of the products and services explain how easy it is to get started.

Note your potential clients may have more than one objection, it's important to be able to identify each one.

Once you know what is stopping the sales process, you can arm yourself with the right arguments.

SUMMARY

- Use a closing question after presenting the solution "Based on what you've told me…".

- Remember objections are part of the sales process and should not be something fearful.

- Overcome the price objection by acknowledging the objection and asking a question, "I appreciate what you're saying but, why do you think it's expensive?."

- Use the same words the customer used in your question above.

- Try to learn the correct order of explaining and drawing the price justification formula.

- Remember to use closing questions and prepare yourself to either close the sale or deal with a hidden objection.

Go practice with someone. Go interact with real customers and see for yourself how it works.

BONUS INFORMATION:

I want to share with you an e-mail thread of a client who used the price objection formula in a unique way. He won a multi-million dollar contract using the technique, in the food manufacturing sector to provide packaging solutions to his client. I have left out the details of the individuals and companies in order to respect their privacy, however, I am sharing the conversation thread with you so you can see how it worked.

Mind you, I recommend doing this price justification formula in person (face to face). This was done over email and was still very much effective! Here it goes:

Salesman: *"Dear (Customer's name), Please review attached quote revised per your request to reflect substrate change for Bobbie 8 count Flexpack. Substrate cost difference from Mett 17 micron to clear 20 micron would realise a 2% cost reduction/kg. I trust this meets with your approval and we can receive your PO accordingly. Regards…"*

Customer: *"Hi (Salesman's name), I am in receipt of your quotation and from all indications given, the pricing difference between metalled and clear packaging is greater than 2%. To be honest I was expecting something closer to the $5 mark. Can you please review as I find it not in line with other suppliers. If need be I can get a quotation from my overseas supplier but I did not think that this would be necessary. Looking forward to your reply. Regards…"*

Salesman: *"Dear (Customer's name), I appreciate your feedback. You believe our cost to be expensive. Let's take a closer look. Our agreed objective, as we begin the relationship, was to qualify our substrates and print for your various applications. We wish to be transparent in our pricing. There is a 4% difference in the clear laminate structure and our raw substrate cost is 50% of the selling price/kg. Overall we are looking at a price difference of $480.00 TTD as per revised quote and your request for $5.00/kg. Would you agree that a local supply with shorter lead times, reducing your inventory level, and local technical support, at that price difference is value beyond the cost? I will call today to speak directly on this. Regards…"*

Customer: *"Dear (Salesman's name), Thanks for your feedback. I agree that you add additional value beyond your cost of materials. However as I have just visited some markets we intend to enter, cost of material is paramount and not insignificant to our competitiveness. As I mentioned, it was not in line however I will accept your pricing for this product as we have to work together to solidify our relationship and to build out our manufacturing sector by creating more valuable clusters of which I am passionate. Please take this as an acknowledgement of the price and (staff member name) will follow up the operational PO part of this. One last note, can you please let me know what other micron structures you have to be able to laminate to? For instance, printed 30 micron clear laminated to 20 micron… 15 micron… etc? This last part is hard to explain so call me if you need clarification. My cell is … Thanks …"*

CHAPTER 6

CLOSING THE SALE

*"You don't close a sale, you open
a relationship if you want to build a
long-term successful enterprise."*
~Patricia Fripp

Closing a sale is simply 'asking the customer to buy'. It is very important to ask for the sale. One of the biggest impediments to sales success is that many people do not ask for the sale. This happens because of fear. More specifically, a fear of rejection. Hence, there is always a constant search for closers in sales recruitment.

By the end of this chapter, you will learn certain techniques that would help you to close a sale in different ways. I have used a number of these techniques over the years and have chosen the ones that works the best for me, depending on the conversation with my customer. You'll know which would be most appropriate in the moment and I assure you, you would have success.

One of my personal colleagues and good friend is Nigel Khan. Nigel is the founder and owner of Nigel R. Khan Booksellers in Trinidad. It is the largest book store brand with numerous locations. I decided to pay Nigel a visit and ask him 'what were his thoughts about closing a sale', when it came to business. What he shared with me was more inspiring and insightful than I expected:

> *Adrian, I believe an important aspect of making a sale is 'relating' to that person, and getting the right vibe out of that person. That person must be able to see themselves in your eyes and see that you hold the power of influence.*
>
> *It's all about stroking someone else's ego while not depreciating yourself. You must look at things from their perspective and be approachable and send out the right, positive vibe. Most people lose confidence in others when they see that they're 'wishy-washy' and not organised.*
>
> *One of the best factors in success and closing a sale is having the confidence and having it all at your fingertips. If you're selling yourself to a bank or any financial institution, if you're selling to a publisher, or your company, it is always an act of publicity and people are*

always judging your every move. Right now, while you're taking this story, you are judging my every movement, every moment of either my strengths or my weaknesses.

You must be relatable and you must be able to laugh at yourself. Some of the key points also is, if you look at people's body language, the person you're dealing with, when they lean 'into' you, you are getting there. When they listen intently, you are getting even closer and then when you're closer at the sale, you 'pull out' and say something like "give me your opinion", that way you will not have them hesitating. Just listen, learn and give them time to compile, and speak.

Then just throw the topic of discussion off, relate about something else. Find key common ground, like, for instance Adrian, you're wearing your Rotary Club shirt right now. Find one common thread that can create a link. Sometimes it could be that they know someone else that you know or a company that you deal with. It's the old Chinese principle of Guanxi (or Guanshi) where they do business by reference and relationships. A lot of people still do business by reference. Historically, people will go with a business partner if he has a good reference or has been recommended by someone. That's how it was done traditionally 'long ago'. People feel more comfortable with someone who is a second or third party recommendation. That's why you must always be visible, whether you are selling books, furniture, cars, you must always be visible, relatable and credible.

Starting with the right vibration and removing people's doubts and risks factors are important because once someone is buying something, if you remove the risk factors of doing business with you by saying "you know what, if it doesn't work" or "if you buy this and it doesn't work, you could bring it back. I guarantee that". People like that personal touch and that personal guarantee that you are willing, and if you could, you would do it. If you go all out and people relate to you in that manner, you'll be successful in closing a sale!

Always look for the eye movement. Always look for the intent stare. Always look at the 'leaning-in'. Always look at credibility and the nodding of the head and being relate-able. The minute you are relatable and they find a common ground with you, the rest is smooth sailing.

But smooth sailing doesn't close there. Because after you sell someone or close the sale, you continue along that path of maintenance of that relationship. You track your relationships with people. I journal a lot so I find out and keep nuances and keep people I deal with whether it's a teacher or a supplier. I will find out and ask something like "how are the kids?" "I heard your daughter is writing exams!" People relate to that and just the thought of a memory or recognition. Our egos need to be massaged.

Let's use a good example of a BMW. People must relate to that salesperson. They must feel comfortable. People may come in and say "My God, I love that car but it's a bit too expensive!" but you in the right context should reply and relate of how it's affordable and the long term effects, the use of the car and how it will impact their life. "It's a quality vehicle and you're a quality person"

Of course you do have the customers from hell. Some customers are deliberately aggressive by coming in to say "no, I need to get this now!" and with that form of aggression, those customers turn out to be your most loyal customers ever. Because the most difficult customers are the ones who have seen you in action. Some of those customers I get along with really well because they are focused, they know what they are about, and they like open, and 'plain talk'.

Nigel emphases heavily on the fact that you cannot close a sale unless you've built a great relationship with people. It is the one mantra that he lives by and I believe it is the one true factor to his success!

Nigel R. Khan is the CEO and Founder of Nigel R. Khan Booksellers, a mentor and inspiration to many people. He has helped many people grow through his work and motivating personality.

Check him out at
www.nigelrkhanbookseller.com

We have established that we already built a relationship with the customer, we asked questions, got information that was important and used it as our ammunition in order to figure out the emotional drive or reason that had a deep meaning for the customer. Then we made a recommendation of our solution/product that suits the customer specifically and was able to overcome the most popular objection of "your price is too high". Not only that, in case the customer didn't realise that something else was holding them back from making a decision (hidden objection), we buried the original price objection and dealt with the new one asking if we met this need, if they'd proceed with their decision.

Now you have to remember that the objection and hidden objections are situational. They don't always happen. But just in case it does happen, you have the tools to deal with them. Let's just say now that you've passed that point.

Either you dealt with objections, or the customer is happy when you asked them the initial closing question when you presented your solution. *"Based on what you've told me, I recommend... does this sound like what you're looking for?"* If they had said yes, what would have been your next step?

You close the sale! But first let's break down the meaning of that phrase 'close a sale'.

Closing a sale is really asking for the sale from the customer. Basically asking the customer to buy. The problem I see with this is that many people take that meaning literally and believe that it is the only way to ask for a sale. Why is that?

Since fear of rejection is one of the biggest impediments to sales success, many people don't actually ask for the business! Hence, there is a constant search for "closers" in sales recruitment!

It is very important to understand from the beginning, that closing in business and sales, is always opening long-term relationships. Never think of it as a task but as a strategy for your success for the rest of your life. Relationships go much longer than the business done. A true testament to this is the relationships I've kept after I left BMW sales, and started my training consultancy. The very same customers who I sold to, were some of my very first customers who hired my services. Had I not given them top-class service back then, I would have struggled in my start-up a whole lot more!

Now there's two things that you could do at this point. You can go straight in for a close and get a commitment or you can play with the customer's emotions for a minute before going in for the close.

Personally, I enjoy playing with the customer's emotions and observe them go on an emotional journey before I let them make the commitment.

This strategy of taking the customer on an emotional journey allows you to remind the customer of where they are right now without your solution and where they would like to be (with your solution). You do not hard sell but make them desire what you have even more by creating and widening this gap in their minds. A distinction from pain-pleasure, from failure-success, from past-future, from where they are now, to where they want to be.

ALIGN THE CLOSE

Aligning the close is setting the customer's mind into the 'buying mode'. I use this most of the time because it really pushes them over the edge into making a commitment. The only time I do not use this strategy is when I realise that the customer's mind is already at that point.

Now this is a five-step process. Is it easy to remember five things? I sure hope so.

If you do these five things and you do it well, you would have that customer happy about making the decision of choosing you. If you don't do it when needed, or don't do it well, the customer can take control of the conversation and you potentially lose the sale, or take really long to gain commitment.

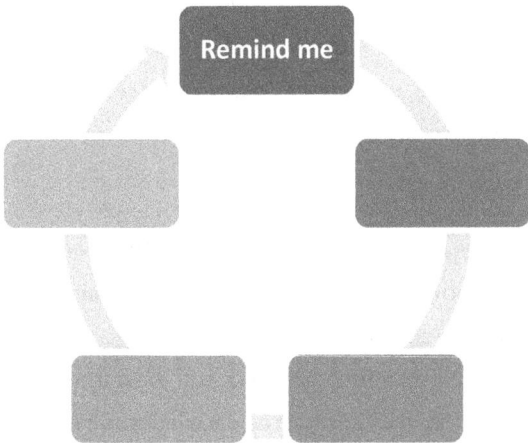

The first part of the five step process is that you need to remind the customer that they have not made a decision as yet, and that they are still in the same position of not having your solution. Which means that they are seeing the same results, which is something that they do not want.

Your language to them here is to speak with them in a way that sounds as if you're recapping your notes from the discussion. But what you're really doing is reminding them that they are not in a good position right now. And you must get them to agree. Getting them to agree actually makes the customer affirm that they are not where they want to be right now. Remind them of that fact and get them to say 'yes' either verbally or non-verbally. It should go like this, for example:

> *"Remind me again. You said that your machinery breaks down at least once a week and the time to get that back up and running takes a couple hours and that makes you lose almost $50,000.00 in business. Is that right?" "Yes!"*

Starting the statement using the words 'Remind me again' makes it sound as if you are recapping your notes, but what you are actually doing is positioning and reminding the customer that they are in a bad position right now. When they say 'yes' and agree to what you've said (what you've said was based on the information discussed when you were asking questions about the current status and discovered the emotional reason), you immediately begin to position them into one end of a gap (where they are now).

Once you get that confirmed 'yes' response from them, that's your que to move on to the second step of the process.

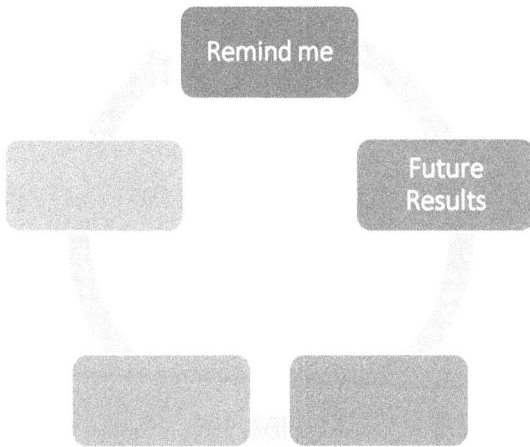

This is the development of the next end of the gap (where they want to be/ results they want to see). What you have to do here is use that information you got from the goals part of the questioning you did earlier on in the process.

Basically, just as if you're recapping your notes and making sure that you 'have the correct information from everything you have discussed, you are going to say something here again regarding that next end of the gap and get a confirmation of a 'yes' response from your customer.

What you do in their mind up to this point is that you have just developed the gap of where they are now vs where they want to be. There would be desire to go to where they want to be. For example:

"Is it right to say then, that with this new equipment (solution presented earlier), you would not have to worry about that much down-time, and as a result increase profits every week? Is that so?" "Yes!"

You've just made them excited about your solution even further. That's the desire. That's the emotions you're playing with at this point!

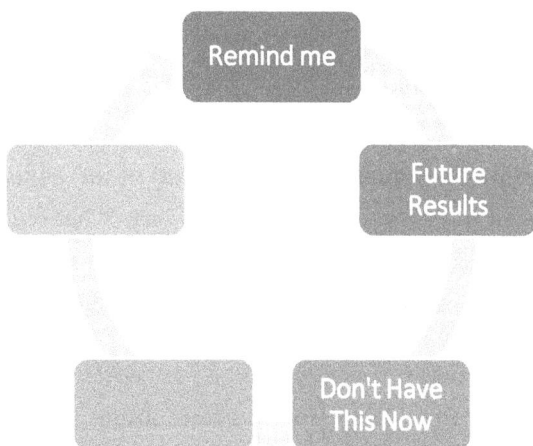

In step one of aligning the close, we made them feel 'bad' about where they are now. In step two, we made them feel good about where they are going (with our solution).

What do you think step three does? Exactly, we make them feel bad again because this is an emotional roller coaster ride you are putting them on. Pull at their heart strings to get them into a mode where they feel like they need to make a decision and act now!

Here's step three. This one is very simple as it is basically one line you say and expect another 'yes' response from your customer.

We make them feel bad again by making reference to step two and remind the customer that they do not have this solution in place right now. For example:

"Would it be fair to say that you don't have this (solution as in step 2) in place right now?" "Yes"

Thinking back on those three steps. Put yourself into the position of the customer and think about how you are feeling. Think about how you feel about me (the salesman). Think about how you feel about the solution offered.

Step four is very important. If done correctly, you would have the customer at such a high emotional state. But if not done effectively, they would still be emotional enough to make a decision, just not at a 'climax' as I would call it. It is very important to use proper tenses and descriptions in this step. This step is the longest of all five but it is the most emotional thing you can possibly do to a customer.

Of course we know this is an emotional roller coaster so this step is a step where you make the customer feel good again. In this case I'd say, feel really good about your solution.

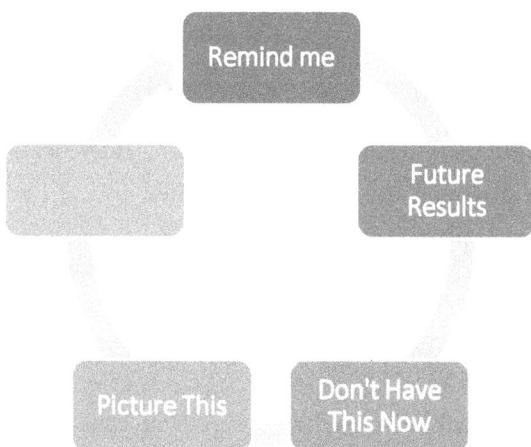

What you do here is describe the 'ideal' situation where the customer has already invested in you and done business with you. They are seeing results of having made that decision. You have to describe it in the 'present tense' so that they can live in that situation in the present moment.

Don't say things like 'would be' or 'would see' or 'would experience'. That's future tense.

You want them to live in the moment. Already having done business with you. If I were to give you an example related to the ones we did in the previous steps, it would go like this:

"Okay, picture this: it is a clear Friday morning and as you walk into your big blue factory doors, you look at the time and you notice it is exactly 9:15a.m. You look to the left where the big grey wall is and notice that all your staff is on the factory floor, and the machinery is up and running at full speed. There are no hiccups. You look to your right where the trucks reverse in for loading, and notice that all the trucks are loading on time. In fact, at that very moment, you realise that you went for the entire week at full production with no delays!"

As you read that situation, did you live in the moment? Did you see the details? The time? The colour of the doors? The wall? The staff? The production line? The truck loading zone?

If you lived in that moment, you understand how the small details play a major role in this step. If you can do this to your customer you would be a winner.

At this point, there is no need for you to get a confirmation from your customer. In fact, they do not even need to say anything at this point. You just need to be observant of their body language. If it looks positive for you, you do the final step which is to ask a question.

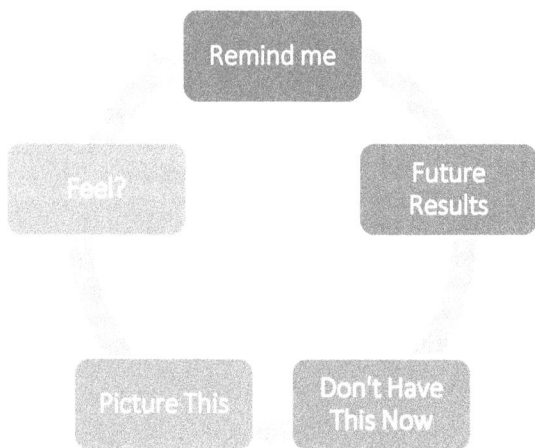

"How do you feel?"

This is an important question after you painted a real time picture of their life/business with your solution already implemented.

The key to this being effective is that after you paint the picture, but before you ask this question, you pause. You pause for a couple reasons.

Firstly, for effect so that the picture you just painted in their minds has had enough time to 'sink in'.

Secondly, to make your observation on their body language, and to ensure that you have given them that roller coaster ride.

Here's a snap shot of the five steps:

> *"Remind me again. You said that your machinery breaks down at least once a week and the time to get that back up and running takes a couple hours and that makes you lose almost $50,000.00 in business. Is that right?" "Yes!"*

> *"Is it right to say then, that with this new equipment (solution presented earlier), you would not have to worry about that much down-time, and as a result increase profits every week? Is that so?" "Yes!"*

> *"Would it be fair to say that you don't have this (solution as in step two) in place right now?" "Yes."*

> *"Okay, so picture this. It is a clear Friday morning and as you walk into your big blue factory doors, you look at the time and you notice it is exactly 9:15a.m. You look to the left where the big grey wall is and notice that all you staff is on the factory floor, and the machinery is up and running at full speed. There are no hiccups. You look to your right where the trucks reverse in for loading, and notice that all the trucks are loading on time. In fact, at that very moment, you realise that you went for the entire week at full production with no delays!"*

> **Pause**

> *"How do you feel?"*

You should try writing one of these based on the product or service that you have to offer. You are ready to close the sale and you know you need to align the close. I would guide you with the starting lines and you now need to finish them with your specific situations to your customers.

"Remind me again. You said,

....
....
....

"Is that right?"

"Yes!"

"Is it right to say then,

....
....
....

"Is that so?"

"Yes!"

"Would it be fair to say that you don't have this in place right now?"

"Yes."

"Okay, picture this:

....
....
....

....

....

....

....

....

Pause

"How do you feel?"

CLOSE THE SALE

As I mentioned before, closing the sale is really asking the customer to buy. Sense the fear of rejection is one of the biggest impediment to sales success, companies always on the constant search for 'closers' in sales recruitment.

At this point I would like to share with you some of the different types of 'closes' that I personally used with great success.

If you use any one of these, depending on the conversation with your customer, you would notice a big change in the way customers respond to you and as a result, close sales more effectively.

Here are my favourite types of closes that helps me get a lot of business.

Direct Close

"Are you ready to make your decision now?" or

"Just sign here."

People fear using this technique because it seems too direct. This is where the fear of rejection comes in and people end up not closing a sale. Use it when you are very sure the customer is ready to buy.

Alternative Choice Close

"Would you prefer to pay with cash or cheque?" Or,

"Would you like the abc system or the xyz?"

This is one of my favourites. I really like to use this when I have more than one option to give to a customer. When a customer selects one of those options, it means they have made the decision to go with that particular option.

Assumptive Close

"Just pass me your credit card and I'll get the paperwork ready." Or, "When would you like the installation?"Here, the salesperson intentionally assumes that the prospect has already agreed to buy, and wraps up the sale or they assume the sale is already made in the customer's mind, and looks past commitment.

Sent Email/Letter

Phone Call

- Introduce
- If it's a Bad time
- Reference to email/letter
- Interesting?
- Set meeting – 2 date options

Start meeting

- Greeting
- Grab Attention

Small Talk

Establish the Objective

- Customer's Benefit
- Agenda
- Anything to add – Continue?

Questions

- Current Status
- Goals/Intentions
- Issues/Barriers
- Consequence

The Minor Point Close

"In whose name should this go under?" Or, "Would the front door look better painted red?

Here, the salesperson deliberately gains agreement with the prospect on a minor point, and uses it to assume that the sale is closed.

The Sharp-Angle Close

Customer: "Are you able to get the system up and running within two weeks?"

Sales Consultant: "If I guarantee it, do we have a deal?"

In this case, this is another one of my favourites. However, only in special cases where the opportunity for this comes up, can it work successfully.

Provide the Solution

- Solution
- Benefits
- Appeal to Emotional Drive

Closing Question

Objection (Optional if there is one)

- Acknowledge Objection
- Take a Closer Look
- Wouldn't you like to save?

Closing Question

- Hidden Objection
- Bury Original Objection
- Would you proceed?

Align the Close

Close the Sale (Choose one close)

The different types of closes that I have seen massive success with, are what I have given to you here. Of course there are many other types that you can use. There are many other resources and world experts where you can learn how to successfully close a sale. I recommend you do more research and find other ways that you can close a sale in your industry. Don't just rely on this book. Always keep learning.

I want to pay close attention to something that many salespeople do and do not realize the effect it has on their customers. Perhaps you have done this yourself and it's possible that it was not effective with some customers. What I want to share with you is a type of close that many salespeople use that turns customers off. I recommend that you don't ever use this going forward.

The Possibility of Loss Close/ Window of Opportunity Close

"The price will increase in a few days." Or, "There's only one more in stock."This approach is mostly over used and abused. Many times this has been used on myself by other people and it really turned me off. I felt as though I was being forced to make a decision, to give them my money, and no matter how much value they built, it seemed to disappear when they used one of these lines on me. Imagine if that is how I'm feeling, imagine what your customer would feel like if you use it on them? We all know that we should do unto others as we would like others to do unto us. Don't make your customer feel uncomfortable before doing business with you (or even after doing business with you!).

SUMMARY

- After presenting the solution or overcoming any objections if they appear, align the close to set the customer into a buying frame of mind.

- Play with their emotions using the information you got when you questioned them.

- Make them feel bad and feel good at the same time.

- Speak in present tense.

- Be very descriptive and pause when necessary.

- Use one of the closes that is most suitable to the situation.

- Research and always learn more.

Go practice with someone. Go interact with real customers and see for yourself how it works.

Note:

*Use this summary layout in all your meetings going forward as a guide to understand how to take your customer to the next step of the sales process.

You can have this in your notes as you take information from your customer during the discussion and it will help you to always keep control of the conversation.

From this point onwards this would be your key points as you would know what you can use, when and where you can use them as well.

I have given you the entire process here in this book. You *do not* need to follow this entire process in all your meetings. Each meeting with a customer is unique. Some sales processes takes one meeting, others take a series of meetings over months before closing a sale. It all depends on the industry you are in, your customer is in, your market or country, what products or services you offer etc.

Don't get carried away and try to follow it exactly and go to each point. Learn to use it as a guide and know how to zig and to zag in any given situation.

CHAPTER 7

RAVING AND LOYAL FANS

*"Customer loyalty should not be based
on compensation, loyalty should be
given unconditionally."*
~ Jim Cathcart

"Customer loyalty is being approached wrongly by the vast majority of people in Business." says Jim Cathcart, who is a Success Consultant and Bestselling Author. He is the creator of the Cathcart Institute, a motivation and sales expert, and a professional speaker. He delivered over 3,000 professional speeches around the world, authored 18books, served as president of the National Speakers Association, inducted into the

International Sales & Marketing Hall of Fame, and have received most of the top awards that professional speakers aspire to receive.

I am eternally grateful, and I feel honoured, for the opportunity to work with Mr. Jim Cathcart. I will share one of his experiences now with you, all of which he shared with me for this book.

> *Jim said to me, "I believe customer loyalty should be given, not pursued."*

It is about you and me, being loyal to our customers, and not about them being loyal to us. Because they have no reason to be loyal to us, but we have every reason to be loyal to them. When it comes to customer loyalty, the question in the salesperson or businessperson's mind should be *"how can I prove to my customers that I value them and I'm loyal to them?"*

Here's the experience Jim had (as told by him):

> *Adrian let me share this with you. "Coffee Bean and Tea Leaf (a company in existence since 1963), is the competitor of Starbucks. They are worldwide, they have a local coffee shop here in Westlake Village California where I've been going since before it became the Coffee Bean and Tea Leaf brand. (More than twelve years). Every time I go in there, I order exactly the same thing. I order the flavour of the day, and oatmeal. Every day, no change.*

I usually bring my business colleagues there for meetings because it's not too far from my home. The coffee shop gets my business, business from my colleagues, not just for coffee but food as well. I frequently have meetings there. As well, I'm part of a hiking group of 60 persons, yeah, 60. We hike every Sunday, Wednesday and Friday. So three days a week, every week, we hike and afterwards we go to The Coffee Bean and Tea Leaf, and overwhelm them with business.

I went in there four or five months ago, and said:

"I'd like a flavour of the day, medium and I'd like and an oatmeal."

They said, "We don't offer the flavour of the day anymore."

"You Don't?" I said, "You've offered it for more than ten years! It's still over there on the shelves in the bags, you can buy them!

"Yeah but we don't brew it anymore."

I said, "Would you brew ME one?"

They said, "No, we don't do that."

"Who decided that?"

"I don't know because it's one of our best sellers!"

"In this store, one of your best selling products was just discontinued, because somebody at the corporate headquarters decided that just wasn't cool?"

She said, "Ya."

I said, "Okay, I won't be coming back."

I left and told my hiking group that I'm no longer going there, so if they continue to go there I'll go somewhere else for breakfast instead of joining the group. Coffee Bean and Tea Leaf lost with one simple decision, and not recognising the message they sent, which was "We know what good coffee is, our customers need to be taught" In other words "we're smart, they're stupid, we'll bring them up to speed". That just means that they don't respect their customers! They discontinued their most popular product and not even respect their store managers to make the right decisions as to whether to offer it or not. They've made it a 'corporate policy' that applies to everybody!

They lost my business, the hiking business group three days a week, they lost their lunch meeting business that I was bringing there and the times I would meet business colleagues for coffee, that's all shifted to different places now. One simple moment of non-loyalty to the customer, and the customer loyalty instantly ended! After more than ten years of my loyalty to them!"

Jim Cathcart was selected as a 2017 Top 25 Speaker (#9) out of 1,300 speakers in an online survey by Speaking.com. This is the 3rd year in a row that Jim achieved this ranking. Designated as the first "Entrepreneur in Residence" by California Lutheran University's School of Management in late 2016. Chosen one of the Top Sales Influencers of 2014, 2015 & 2016 by Top Sales World Magazine based in London & Paris. In December of 2012 Jim Cathcart was inducted into the Sales & Marketing Hall of Fame in London, England. This is in addition to his existing Speaker Hall of Fame listing.

I recommend you visit his website www.cathcart.com to get a copy of at least one of his books.

What Jim's experience tells us is, if we have customers and we are loyal to them, it means we are loyal to them whether or not they are sending us money!

Being loyal to your customers refers to loyalty that is not based on compensation. It's like you love your children even when they misbehave, you don't like when they misbehave, but you love them anyway. Your love is unconditional, so too should your customer loyalty be unconditional Except for the times a customer may behave so obnoxiously, that you may not want them as a customer.

In any type of business a very important factor that determines success is customer loyalty. Customer loyalty is the driving force that brings in repeat business. The reason why customer loyalty matters is that selling more to current customers is easier and cheaper than finding or selling to new ones. They tend to buy more, more frequently and they will recommend your business.

Here are some tips that will assist you in maintaining customer loyalty. I have personally used these over the years and have reaped the benefits of relationships, success and best of all in a financial way. I recommend that you too can use these techniques an experience similar results.

Reach Out

Make time to reach out to your existing customers. It is possible that you haven't heard from them in a while. It could also be that everything is fine. Perhaps, it could also be possible that they have been struggling and haven't really thought about reaching out to you for help. If you call your customer on your own and it so happens that they do have a problem, and you are able to quickly resolve that problem you would be that customer's new hero.

Resolve

Not only if you are able to resolve a customer issue and become the new hero, we need to keep in mind that if we are able to quickly resolve any issues efficiently, only then would we begin to understand that *customer loyalty is strongly tied to the amount of effort that is put in when it comes to resolving a problem*. A customer who can quickly and easily have any issues resolved is far more likely to stay loyal than a customer who has never experienced a problem at all. This is very important to understand because it is much easier for a customer who has never experienced a problem to begin shopping for new products and services elsewhere. But if they were a customer who had experience the problem that you resolved quickly and efficiently, they are less likely to go out shopping because they would be uncomfortable not knowing if they would be able to get the same level of service elsewhere.

Rejoice

If a customer calls with a problem you should be happy. You should celebrate knowing that this is an opportunity to show the customer that their problem can be resolved quickly, and bet your bottom dollar that they would buy from you again.

Renew

Always renew old relationships. Stay in touch with customers after the sale has closed so that you can encourage them to reach out with a problem. The thing is that you may end up spending some extra time doing this, but you might save your customers some pain and the reward would be in the form of future purchases, future business, even referrals of friends and business colleagues.

In delivering exceptional customer service there are a number of things that we must always do throughout the sales process as well as after we have closed the sale. I'm going to share number of these things with you and I hope that you would take note of them and begin practicing them from today.

Smile. If someone is not smiling, give them your smile. I've always heard that a smile is contagious. Early on in life when I learnt this, I tried it just as an experiment and to my surprise, it would work every single time

As Dale Carnegie once said, "The sweetest most important sound anyone can hear is their name,"; and I couldn't agree more. Always try to remember someone's name when you meet them. Repeat it and I promise you, when you see them next time and you call them by name, look at how their face lights up!

Remember to be a good listener and encourage customers to talk about themselves because people love to talk about things that they are interested in. Let the customers do most of the talking. Ask a lot of questions so that you can get a great deal of information that you can use as ammunition to help that customer. Talk in terms of their interest and most importantly be authentic, and genuinely interested in that person.

Asking for a Referral

Many times I see a lot of sales people and young/new or aspiring entrepreneurs asking for a referral at the wrong time. Why do I say it's the wrong time, well they either don't get one or if they do, it's a weak link who probably wouldn't buy. There's a time and place for this. This is very important because in order to get excellent referrals, we need to do good things first. Give good service. Good service goes a long way in this world because we all crave that 'value for money' aspect of business. Why give bad service and expect to get more business? It doesn't work that way.

After you have delivered your product or service and have given the customer excellent service only then should you ask for a referral.

We must never ask for referral *before* we close a sale, give great service or even resolve a painful issue for the customer. When a customer knows that you have given them significant value they would return the favour through referrals. If you know you have done this and you want to ask for a referral, then you are free to do so.

How do we ask for a referral? Many times I hear sales people use a line like this:

> *"Hi, are you able to give me some names of persons who you think would benefit from my product/service?"*

Imagine someone asking you that question. Is it difficult to think of someone? Do you feel pressured into giving them a name? Isn't this an uncomfortable feeling?

Now that I've put you into the customer's shoes and you understand how they feel let's try this differently.

> *"Based on your experience with us, on a scale of 1 to 10 how would you rate your experience?"*

If you got a nine or a 10 only then should you ask for a referral. But, you need to help the customer in giving you those names.

> *"Would you give me the names of one or two persons who you believe would appreciate this new system integrated into the business? It could be a business colleague or a family member."*

By giving the customer two groups of persons from which they can select names, it helps them sort in their minds the people that they know, and this would help them think of someone much faster than if you would to ask just for a name.

If you get a rating of anything eight and under, I recommend that you ask, not for a referral, but for suggestions on how you can improve your service to them for the 'next time'. Customers will tell you what to do. They would have no problem in expressing how they feel you can do a better job. The key thing about this is that you should take their advice and do it. You'd be surprised with the responses you'd get from them when you take action.

Give and You Shall Receive

I have another experience that Jim Cathcart shared with me in a recent conversation we had. Customer loyalty is very important to him, a very close subject, and he takes pride in it. He enjoys working with so many other people just as I do, in improving customer service and the lives of everyone we meet. Here's the story as told by him again:

> I had a customer who hired me years ago. I was in Oklahoma. I got a call from a man named Ben Blackstock, and he said, "Jim, you're 125 miles away, we're in Oklahoma City and I'm with the Oklahoma

Press Association, and we're having a meeting today and our speaker just cancelled, can you fill in?"

I asked, "When's the meeting?"

"Noon."

I said, "Uhhh uh, yeah."

I ran home, put on a suit, jumped in my car drove to Oklahoma City, went to his meeting (I had done some research to prepare myself), and gave the speech that went over well. I shook hands, handed out some business cards and went away. I went back home and that was the last I saw of Ben for a long time. Actually, that was the last time I ever saw him in person in my life! Now this was back in 1979/80.

I would occasionally write an article or newsletter or something, that I thought was worth sharing and I kept Ben's card and so I would send him a copy of these things in the mail. Something short, latest news, like once or twice a year. But I stayed in touch with him.

Then I moved from Oklahoma to California, and formed a partnership with a colleague in San Diego Dr. Tony Alessandra. I was there in my new office two years later and the phone rang, where I answered it. "Hi, this is Jim Cathcart."

"Hi Jim, this is Michael Redwine from Amsterdam Holland. We're interested in some sales training and my boss is coming to the United States to interview sales trainers, could he come and visit with you in San Diego?"

His name was Peter Kutemann and he shows up in his pin striped suit and moustache, looking a little bit younger than me, delightful and intelligent guy, high achiever, representing a company that works internationally. A quite of 'out-of-the-ordinary' kind of business.

Peter was in my office and I eventually asked him, "How did you learn about me?"

He said, "Michael Redwine."

"Well how did Michael Redwine learn about me?"

He said, "His father-in-law in Oklahoma City, Ben Blackstock. He was talking with him and asked if he knew any sales trainers in the United States, and he said "there's one guy who impressed me six years ago, Jim Cathcart."

The Internet wasn't around at that time and Michael didn't know how to reach me. He started calling people trying to find me, and luckily discovered I was in California and called me there.

After that meeting, I was booked six times to places like, Monte Carlo, Scotland, Holland, Belgium even France! OH, my God, all of this from Peter's company came because of one simple thing where I was loyal to a non-paying, one time customer in Oklahoma. I made a lot of money out of that one time help!

Peter and I kept in touch and remained friends and one day after a couple years, he called me and he said, "Hey, I have some engineers that need to be better at dealing with English-speaking people. If I were to fly to the United States in my private Citation-Ten jet, and pick you up and fly to Toulouse France, would you do a seminar for them at your full international fee?"

All of these things came because of customer loyalty. It came from one free speaking event that was inconvenient for me but, because I wanted to do something good, for the Oklahoma Press Association.

Jim's experience here teaches us about giving. Have you ever heard the saying, "Ask and you shall receive?" Well, not all the time that works out or comes to pass the way we as humans want it to. But what I am going to say is that Jim's experience on giving teaches us, "Give, and you shall receive."

SUMMARY

- Arouse an eager want in customer.

- Make them feel important.

- Get the other person to agree immediately.

- Make the other person happy about your solution.

- Dramatise your ideas.

- Show respect for customer's opinion.

- Never say 'you're wrong'.

- If you are wrong admit quickly and continue.

- Ask the customer about their experience with you and to rate you out of 10.

- If you get a nine or 10, then ask for a referral.

- If you get anything eight and under, ask for their suggestion on what you can do to improve their experience next time.

Be loyal to your customers first, and in turn their loyalty will pay off for you the same way it did for me, and same way it did for everyone you read about in this book.

Just as Robin Sharma says, "Produce like Picasso, lead like Mandela, live like Branson". If you believe that sales is equal to income, I recommend following the techniques in this book and start using them daily. Print the summary flow and use that as your daily guide to control the flow of the conversations you would have with your customers to win new business every day. I believe in you. I also believe that with persistent, consistent determination, a will to succeed and achieve, and by taking action towards your goals, you can do this! You can succeed in sales and in life!

Are you going to take that step from today?

Carpe Diem

Adrian N. Havelock